Mediaeval Education and the Reformation

Mediaeval Education and the Reformation

by John Lawson

Senior Lecturer in Education
University of Hull

LONDON

ROUTLEDGE AND KEGAN PAUL

NEW YORK : HUMANITIES PRESS

First published 1967
by Routledge and Kegan Paul Ltd
Broadway House, 68–74 Carter Lane
London, E.C.4

Printed in Great Britain
by Northumberland Press Limited
Gateshead on Tyne

© John Lawson 1967

Library of Congress Catalog Card Number 67-18839

Contents

CONTENTS

Foreword

There has long been a need for a straightforward account of the early development of English education. Study of its history often begins only with the nineteenth century, as if this marked the beginnings of state intervention and of the shaping of educational institutions in accordance with social needs. Mr. Lawson, who is the author of an excellent history of a local grammar school, makes it clear that the schools and universities of the mediaeval period arose to meet the social needs of that time. He follows developments up to the sixteenth century when the Reformation brought profound social and religious changes which necessarily affected education very closely at many points, not only the organization of schools and universities but also the curriculum. Indeed, this was a turning point when the foundations of an educational system, in the modern sense of the term, were laid.

This account will, therefore, be of interest to all students of education and those who wish to pursue the subject further will find many points of interest to follow up.

BRIAN SIMON

Preface

This short book makes no claim to originality and its dependence on the work of others will be easily apparent. All that has been attempted is to provide for students an outline of present knowledge and opinion about the beginnings of our oldest educational institutions, grammar schools and universities, and their development and expansion under the impact of the Reformation into a rudimentary system of education— the genesis of our present one.

Like all other branches of history, the history of education must ultimately rest primarily on documents, and a new selection of source material for students' use is badly needed. In the absence of any other collection I have given references wherever possible to A. F. Leach's *Educational Charters and Documents* (1911) so that those who wish may see the sort of evidence on which our knowledge rests.

For suggestions and corrections I owe thanks to Professor Brian Simon, Dr. S. H. Atkins, Dr. D. L. Douie and Mr. F. J. Dwyer; for any remaining imperfections I am alone responsible. My chief obligation is to my wife, as always.

J.L.

May, 1966

The grammar master and his scholars.
From John of Garlandia's Vocabulary, printed by
Richard Pynson, 1503. By permission of
the Huntingdon Library, California, U.S.A.

I

Introduction

The English educational system becomes intelligible only in the light of its past, yet the greatest obstacle to our seeing it as it really was in the past is our absorption in the present. We now take for granted state-provided, free and compulsory education; highly organized schools with hundreds of pupils, expensive buildings and equipment, and staffs of trained and specialist teachers with guaranteed salaries and pensions; and somewhere in the background organizers, inspectors, administrators, examining boards, teacher-training institutions, professional associations and so on. But all this is relatively recent—a development of the past century or so. Every system of education is a living growth within the society it serves, and our present system is the product of an age of democracy and social welfare, of material prosperity and state control.

Mediaeval education was utterly different because it developed in a social order that was utterly different. It was the outcome of assumptions and ways of life which our present milieu makes it hard for us to imagine, though some of our present educational institutions—our oldest grammar schools and universities—have descended to us, albeit much changed, from those times.

I

Before we can begin to understand what mediaeval education was like we must appreciate some of the fundamental differences between mediaeval and twentieth-century society.

First, the state which now dominates education then had no interest in it at all. Comparatively, the mediaeval state was a poor and rudimentary thing, concerned with little but law and order and the taxation necessary for their support; government and politics can very seldom have touched the lives of ordinary people, least of all those living in remote rural areas. To a much greater extent than now life was ordered by religion and the Church. All Englishmen were Catholics until the mid-sixteenth century, and in an age of faith and ecclesiastical authority the Church was an ever-present influence in men's affairs.

But the most striking features of mediaeval education spring less from differences in the comparative rôles of Church and state in people's lives than from differences in population and social welfare. Because of starvation, pestilence and medical ignorance the population was small; it increased very slowly from about a million or a million and a half in 1100 to about three and a half millions in 1348; but then it was catastrophically reduced, perhaps by as much as 40 per cent, by the Black Death, and it had barely reached three millions again by 1500. More people now live in the West Riding than ever lived in the whole of England at any time in the middle ages. Moreover, whilst our society is urban, industrial and affluent, our ancestors' was rural, agrarian and poverty-stricken. It was also based on gross inequalities. The vast majority of people lived in small, remote villages, hamlets or scattered farmsteads, and whether free or unfree wrested a precarious subsistence

2

from the ground by unremitting toil. Life was stark and primitive, a harsh struggle for existence against famine and disease, and every member of the family was involved almost as soon as he was old enough to scare the crows or weed the fields.

In these conditions schooling was out of the question for most children; but that is not to say they were uneducated. Education consisted not of book-learning acquired in school but of religious beliefs and moral values instilled in church, of vocational skills learnt whilst following the plough or watching in the byre, of the ancient customs and superstitions of the country-side heard in the firelight on winter nights. All mediaeval education, even the most bookish, was practical and vocational: that given in schools was for a small minority of persons who needed to be able to read and write Latin, though as material prosperity and leisure increased in the later middle ages schooling of this kind became commoner among people who were not intended to be clerks in the professional sense. The modern idea that all children, more or less, should go to the same kind of school, should enjoy equality of educational opportunity and the right to develop their capacities to the full, irrespective of family circumstances—this would have been incomprehensible to the mediaeval mind: it would have undermined the whole of society.

For whilst we now accept education as a rightful means of social mobility, mediaeval society was based on stability: every man had his God-given station, and the social order was relatively static. Certainly, peasants' sons sometimes received school education, but since this was a means of escape from the soil and therefore a loss to their lord, his permission had to be

3

bought by fine, and fourteenth-century manorial rolls record numerous instances of this. The sole purpose of manumission by this means was to allow villeins' sons to take holy orders, and theoretically their freedom lapsed if they failed to become clerics—there was no question of education promoting social mobility in a general way. Even this practice was regarded as socially harmful, and in 1391 the Commons petitioned the king in Parliament 'to ordain . . . that no serf or villein henceforward put his children to school, in order to procure their advancement by clergy'. Only after 1406, with the Statute of Apprentices, could a villein send his children to school without let or hindrance.[1] Thus, whilst mediaeval man would have admitted that everybody needed training in the practical work he had to do, he would have regarded schools as providing this only for clerks—those concerned in one way or another with books and writing. 'The idealism which in the middle ages corresponded to our educational idealism,' observes Sir Maurice Powicke, 'was nothing more nor less than the desire that every man should live the good life and do honestly what God had given him to do.' And that remained the generally accepted view of those in authority until not so very long ago.

Education in the middle ages inevitably reflected these conditions. There was no organized system of schools: in most cases their provision was a matter of chance. Schools with a permanent existence were few and mostly in towns; elsewhere they tended to be sporadic and intermittent. London with a relatively large and wealthy population of some 50,000 had five established schools in 1446. A moderately-sized town of 2,000 inhabitants might contain no more than 20 or 30 boys whose parents could afford book-learning. An

4

isolated village with 10 or 12 families would not muster enough children to warrant a school, even if poverty had not precluded one. Thus, a well-established town school with a continuous existence might consist of no more than two or three dozen boys taught by one master in a single room. Any other kind of school was little more than a group of children with a teacher meeting in any available room. Clearly then if we equate mediaeval schools with present-day ones—in large buildings, with separate classes and a staff of teachers—we miss the point entirely. Similarly, we are misled if we suppose any clear distinction between 'elementary' or 'primary' and 'secondary' education—these are modern categories. Most schools were grammar schools, i.e. they taught Latin; but in the later middle ages growing prosperity brought into being reading and writing schools in towns to serve the needs of the trading class. Where there was a village school it would more resemble our Sunday schools, and consist of a priest or parish clerk teaching the rudiments of the faith to a group of young children, perhaps in some corner of the church. These remote and humble schools must have had a casual existence and they have left behind little or no trace. The schools we know most about are the grammar schools, and about them we know little enough.

This last point needs to be borne in mind. Because of lack of evidence our knowledge of much in mediaeval education is very incomplete. This applies particularly to the distribution and continuity of schools. Documentary references are often slight and fortuitous, indicating no more than that there was a school in a certain place at a certain time. Usually it is not a school but a schoolmaster that is mentioned, perhaps in a rental or as a witness to a lease or a conveyance. In 1496, in an inquiry before the archbishop of York's court concerning the parochial use of the nave of Kirkham priory church in the East Riding, a witness aged 38 attested that as a child he had attended a school in the nave very near the font—he remembered throwing stones at the 'litle steeple' on the font cover.[2] This chance allusion is the only evidence we have that there was a school in this village in the 1460s, or at any other time in the middle ages.

II

Schools in mediaeval England

Anglo-Saxon beginnings

Schools were probably first established in England with the coming of Christianity. When St. Augustine and his band of monks arrived at Canterbury from Rome in 597 to convert the men of Kent an early object would be to train native priests, and we may suppose that a school would be established almost as soon as a church. The same assumption may be made of his coadjutors who soon afterwards founded cathedrals at Rochester and London, and in 627 at York. No records prove the existence of these early schools; they are inferred from the practice of the Church in Italy and Gaul where each bishop provided personally for the training of his clergy.

Thus, the first schools in England were Latin or grammar schools founded by the Church. They taught Latin because that was the language of the Church in all its services, and also because everything that was then known and in writing was in Latin. For most of the next thousand years the word school almost invariably meant a grammar school: its chief function was to supply the Church with clergy and it was usually located near if not actually within the church itself.

Religion continued to be the nursing mother of education until the nineteenth century.

The pioneer historian of England's mediaeval schools was A. F. Leach, who died in 1915. His industry was enormous and he did a giant's work among previously unexploited records, so much so that every subsequent historian of English schools has stood on his shoulders. But because he had a case to prove he was prone to prejudice and overstatement, as well as being unduly aggressive in controversy.[3] Leach was emphatic in asserting the continuity of these early schools. That it was the present King's School at Canterbury which St. Augustine had allegedly founded c 600, and that St. Peter's at York was the very school supposedly established by St. Paulinus in 627 he had no doubt whatever. Not only is this an opinion for which proof does not exist, it also lacks credibility.[4]

Leach also had a bias against monks which made it hard for him to credit them with any services to education. In this he was plainly wrong, at least for the Anglo-Saxon period. Monasticism, deriving partly from Celtic Ireland, was a power in the religious and educational revival inaugurated by Archbishop Theodore in the late seventh century, and its leading scholars and teachers were monks, like Aldhelm and Bede. Again, in the tenth century, following the devastations of the Danes, monasticism promoted the restoration of religion and learning, the outstanding educator of the age being the schoolmaster-monk Aelfric.

Although the purpose of education was essentially to teach future priests what they needed to know for the Christian ministry, some secular knowledge was indispensable. This was traditionally composed of the 'Seven Liberal Arts', and these came to be divided into the

8

more elementary *trivium* and the more advanced *quadrivium*. The *trivium* consisted of grammar, rhetoric and logic, and formed the substance of school education; the *quadrivium* consisted of music, arithmetic, geometry and astronomy, and this formed the framework of such advanced training as there was until the twelfth century. The texts in which these subjects were studied were compendiums of ancient learning made in the fifth and sixth-century twilight of the Roman world by Martianus Capella, Boethius and Cassiodorus, the first two of whom were to be standard authorities for a thousand years.

So far as we know, scholastic activity remained predominantly monastic until the twelfth century, when it gradually passed to the new secular cathedral schools and the emergent universities. But evidence for Anglo-Saxon education is so meagre that generalization is dangerous. How numerous schools were and how continuously they existed, or how many and what sort of pupils they had, there is no means of knowing. Almost certainly their main purpose was to train boys to become priests or monks; any other pupils they had were probably few and limited to the upper class. The great mass of people, and perhaps most of the clergy too, can have been little touched by them. Our information about these schools is so scanty that they may best be regarded merely as a prelude to the later history of education for which records are progressively more numerous.

The twelfth-century renaissance

The true beginnings of mediaeval and therefore of modern education—for the development has been broadly continuous—are to be found in the twelfth century. This was a period of intense mental excitement, restless, creative, productive of great changes in religious and intellectual life and education, and one of the turning points of history. The main source of this twelfth-century renaissance was northern France, where scholastic activity ran at fever heat. A surge of religious revivalism which accompanied this intellectual ferment brought into being new religious orders which spread from France throughout western Europe. Cathedrals, built in the new gothic architecture being evolved out of romanesque, were reorganized on a collegiate basis with chapters of secular canons, and became centres of education and learning. Justice and government, both in the Church and in the developing states of the West, were deeply affected by the recovery of the Civil Law containing the legal wisdom of the Romans, and also by the formulation of an authoritative body of ecclesiastical or Canon Law, both initiated by jurists in Bologna. These two legal systems soon became important—and lucrative—subjects of higher education throughout western Christendom. Learning was also stimulated by growing contacts with the Islamic world in Spain, Sicily and the Levant, whereby arabic numerals, algebra and the *Elements* of Euclid were gradually introduced into the West, and valuable additions made to medical and scientific knowledge through Latin translations of ancient Greek authorities which had been preserved in Arabic. Quite the most influential of these was Aristotle, whose logic, now rediscovered in full, intensified the study of dialectics and led to the scholastic method of analysis and argument which shaped all later mediaeval thinking.

The focal points in higher educational activity during this period were the cathedral schools of northern

France, notably those at Laon, Paris and Chartres, where famous masters like Anselm, Abelard and William of Conches attracted large audiences. A new species of wandering scholars appeared—young men craving to learn, tramping from one centre to another in search of knowledge and argument. Some of them were improvident, licentious, blasphemous and semi-pagan, like the 'goliards', as revealed in their Latin songs and satires; but others were genuine scholars, some of whom later rose to eminence in the Church. In England similar schools emerged at Exeter, Salisbury, London and Lincoln—not permanent institutions so much as chance assemblies of scholars gathered round particular masters, like the theologian Robert Pullen who lectured at Exeter before 1133. Any one of these might have developed into England's first university.

Cathedral and collegiate-church schools

Reorganized by the new Norman bishops after the Conquest, the English cathedrals remained unchanged until 1540. Eight of them—Canterbury, Carlisle, Durham, Ely, Norwich, Rochester, Winchester and Worcester—were cathedral priories served by monks, the bishop being also abbot, an arrangement peculiar to England. The other nine—Chichester, Exeter, Hereford, Lichfield, Lincoln, London, Salisbury, Wells and York—conformed to the continental type and were each governed by a chapter of secular canons with four 'dignitaries'—dean (the head of the establishment), precentor, schoolmaster (*scholasticus* or *magister scholarum*) and treasurer. When Archbishop Thomas of Bayeux reconstituted York on this Norman plan *c* 1090 the schoolmaster was the first dignitary to be created, and this probably marks the real beginning of the present St. Peter's School.[6] Thus a school was an important adjunct of these remodelled cathedrals from the beginning. Some cathedral schools, as we have seen, attracted older students at first and might have become universities, but after the development of Oxford and Cambridge in the early thirteenth century they became grammar schools, and our oldest existing schools descend from them. In 1179 the Third Lateran Council ordered every cathedral to provide a schoolmaster to teach the clerks of the church and other poor scholars *gratis*, a decree reiterated by the Fourth Lateran Council of 1215.[7] But in the English cathedrals this seems to have been already common practice.

During the later twelfth century the cathedral *scholasticus* acquired legal and secretarial responsibilities which made him delegate the teaching of the grammar school to a deputy, the schoolmaster or *magister scholarum*, whilst he himself assumed the more impressive style of chancellor. Besides appointing the master and being responsible for the school, the chancellor had other educational functions. To ensure that the school prospered he granted the master a monopoly of grammar-teaching in the city, thus protecting his livelihood from competing rivals. He administered any endowments the school might receive. He was responsible also for licensing other schoolmasters beyond the confines of the cathedral city, presumably to test their orthodoxy; and in some cases he appointed them within the archdeaconry or even the diocese, though the practice seems to have varied.[8]

Grammar masters were to be maintained not only by cathedrals but also (according to the Fourth Lateran's decree) by other churches which could afford it. This meant, in practice, by the greater collegiate churches: those governed by chapters of canons or priests living together on the same foundation, like a cathedral chapter but not housing the seat (*cathedra*) of a bishop. With characteristic certitude Leach declared, 'There can be no manner of doubt . . . that all the cathedral and collegiate churches kept schools, and that the schoolmaster was one of the most important of their officers, and school teaching one of the most important of their functions.'[9] About the cathedrals and similar great churches this is probably true. The three important churches of Beverley, Ripon and Southwell in the diocese of York each had a grammar school (but whether continuously from their Anglo-Saxon foundation, as Leach asserted, is quite beyond proof); so had certain lesser colleges of priests of later foundation, for instance St. Mary's Warwick, Westbury upon Trym in Gloucestershire, Ottery St. Mary in Devon; so had some relatively poor foundations like Howden in the East Riding, Rushford in Norfolk and Wye in Kent. But it is only an inference that a grammar school was the invariable concomitant of every collegiate church.

For whom were these schools maintained? Primarily, in the case of the greater ones, for the instruction of the younger priests and deacons, the vicars choral, clerks and choristers of the establishment, and also for the boys of the neighbourhood whether intended for holy orders or not. To generalize from particular examples where more documentary evidence exists, it appears that the schoolhouse was provided by the chapter, usually near the church but sometimes (as at Lincoln) well in the city for ease of access, the master being responsible for repairs. There is little indication of numbers attending. At York, where the cathedral school may reasonably be supposed to have been comparatively large a testator in 1369 bequeathed 2d to each of 60 pupils, 'not being bad boys', whom the master should name to say the psalter at the donor's obsequies. On the other hand at the grammar school attached to the collegiate church of Mettingham in Suffolk there were only 14 boys in 1535. No doubt in most cases numbers were small enough for the master to teach the school unaided.

About these schoolmasters little is discoverable. They were appointed and licensed by the cathedral chancellor, who must have kept records of them, though very few of these survive. When the chancellor's place was vacant his right passed to the chapter and then appointments are recorded in the chapter act books. Despite the difficulty of tracing continuity there seems no reason to doubt the regular succession of grammar masters, at least in the greater churches.[10] The master might be required by the statutes, as at York, to be an M.A., and his appointment was usually for a term of years only, normally three, so that he could be removed if unsatisfactory. He seems to have received a stipend from the chancellor for those of his pupils who were on the foundation, but charged fees for the others; and no doubt it was to maximize his income from fees that he was granted a local monopoly, which the chancellor enforced even to the extent of excommunicating contumacious rivals. Within a space of eighteen months between 1304 and 1306 the Beverley chancellor silenced three unlicensed grammar masters teaching to the prejudice of the minster school, one actually in the town, the others some five and twelve miles away. Though ordinarily expected to follow the choir and deputize for the chancellor in his absence, the master was not necessarily a priest and sometimes was married. Some were evidently men of civic standing, important enough to be buried in the cathedral church, like Master Richard Burghehill, whose monumental brass in Hereford cathedral still invites the visitor's prayers for his soul.

In the eight monastic cathedrals the situation was different. Here, there was no chapter and no chancellor, and responsibility for schools belonged to the bishop. The general custom—though exceptions occur—was that the bishop appointed schoolmasters in the diocese; and the grammar school, which corresponded to the secular cathedral's, was provided by the bishop for his cathedral city, often being known as the city school (*scola civitatis Cantuariensis, scola civitatis Norwicensis*, for instance). Since this was the bishop's school, the monastery had nothing to do with it, and it stood well within the city whose educational needs it served. At Canterbury the archbishop's school was probably established by the first Norman archbishop Lanfranc c 1085, but nothing is known of it until 1259. Subsequent records show the archbishops appointing successive masters and using the threat of excommunication to protect their monopoly.[11] It is from this school, not the primordial schools of Augustine and Theodore, that the present King's School is descended.

TOWN SCHOOLS

Latin was the language not only of the Church and the learned professions associated with it but also of trade and administration. All business and legal transactions, records, minutes and accounts were written in Latin. Clearly, then, no town of any importance could manage without a supply of clerks able to read and write the language, and this meant a grammar school. Hence where there was no great church to maintain a school the burgesses would be obliged to provide one in their own interests. Perhaps this took the form of offering inducements to a schoolmaster to settle in the town— a rent-free room in which to teach, and a local monopoly to ensure him a competent livelihood from fees. The monopoly, deriving from church licence or town ordinance, was a chief support of the schoolmaster's position; as Coulton noted, 'The right to keep a school was then a privilege as exclusive, and sometimes almost as lucrative, as the landlord's right to keep a mill or an oven'.[12] When borough or other local records associate a schoolmaster with a town where no large church provided a school, one supported in some way or other by the bailiffs and commonalty may be indicated, as for example at Lancaster and Nottingham in the late thirteenth century. In fifteenth-century Hull the mayor and burgesses allowed their schoolmaster not only a monopoly but also a room in which to teach, a dwelling house and at different periods a livery and a salary, and they fixed the fees he might charge. The burgesses of Richmond in Yorkshire were paying their schoolmaster a salary in 1548. In towns where no similar public support was given it is reasonable to assume a private schoolmaster teaching for fees and with a monopoly safeguarded by his licence, though his stay would depend on a continuing demand affording him a sufficient living. There must have been many grammar masters of this kind whose existence has gone unrecorded.

CHANTRY SCHOOLS

To provide a schoolmaster with a guaranteed income

independently of fees, it became common from the late fourteenth century to associate teaching with a chantry. Mediaeval charity was largely inspired by the Catholic belief in the efficacy of prayers for the dead, and by people's desire to provide perpetual intercession for the souls of benefactors and relations; and a chantry was really any foundation having this object. Chantries were usually founded by successful men in the parish church of their native town, and consisted of lands or tenements vested in trustees or patrons, the rents supplying a salary for a priest to pray or celebrate for the founder and those in whom he was interested. Besides his duties at the altar the priest was often required to teach a school, without charging fees since he received a living from the endowment; and there is no doubt that in some founders' minds this educational purpose was as important as the more purely spiritual one. An early example is Lady Katharine Berkeley's chantry school founded in 1384 at Wotton-under-Edge in Gloucestershire, where the chaplain had not only to celebrate in the parish church or the chapel of the foundress's manor house for her, her children, her late husbands and parents, but also, assisted by two scholar-clerks, to teach grammar without taking fees in a schoolhouse newly built for this purpose in the town.[13] In the fifteenth century the foundation of chantries with schools attached became a common expression of charity and piety. Stockport grammar school was thus established by a London alderman and goldsmith in 1488; Skipton in the West Riding by a local rector, some time before 1492; and Macclesfield in 1502 by another London alderman, by trade a merchant taylor.

In some places it was not a new school that the chantry founded, but an already existing one that it endowed. Thus, after 1472 the town school at Lancaster was taught by the priest of a chantry endowed in the parish church by a former mayor; and in 1479 the corporation's school at Hull was similarly provided for by a chantry founded in the town church by Bishop Alcock of Worcester, a native of Hull. In such cases schools which had charged fees usually became free. Lacking an individual benefactor the burgesses themselves, in their corporate capacity, might establish a chantry with the object of supporting a school, as at East Retford in Nottinghamshire *c* 1518. At Richmond in Yorkshire the schoolmaster seems to have served a chantry unconnected with his school, no doubt to augment his stipend from the town, and this may have been common elsewhere.

Whilst the single chaplain was the norm, chantry foundations took other forms. There might be two or more priests living together as a college, one or more of them bound to keep a school. Bishop Thomas Langley of Durham founded a chantry of two chaplains in the galilee of his cathedral in 1414 and built a schoolhouse on Palace Green in which one was to teach grammar, the other song. Archdeacon Sponne's chantry at Towcester, established in 1448, provided for two, one a preacher, one a schoolmaster. About 1510 an alderman of King's Lynn endowed a college of three priests in St. Margaret's church, one of them expressly to teach school. The predominance of the educational motive is obvious in two Yorkshire foundations each consisting of three priest-schoolmasters teaching grammar, song and writing respectively—Acaster College near Selby established *c* 1470 by a bishop of Bath and Wells, and Jesus College, Rotherham, created by Archbishop Thomas Rotherham of York in 1483.

18

Gild and hospital schools

Some schools were maintained by religious institutions which were more than chantries but which still embodied the chantry idea of intercession. Gilds were societies of layfolk formed for particular spiritual or social purposes which often included the employment of a stipendiary chaplain, one of whose duties besides altar service might be to keep a school for the children of members and others. The grammar school at Ludlow was supported by the Palmers' gild; at Louth by the Trinity gild; the Holy Cross gild was responsible for the school at Stratford-on-Avon where the ancient half-timbered schoolhouse and gildhall adjoining the gild chapel still survive. The Trinity gild at Worcester supported the bishop's city grammar school and housed it in their gildhall.

Another religious and charitable institution which sometimes promoted education though existing primarily for another purpose was the hospital or almshouse, endowed for the care of the sick and aged poor. Several hospitals, at certain periods if not continuously, boarded grammar-school boys—St. Giles at Norwich, Gaunt's at Bristol, St. John the Baptist at Exeter and Ripon, for example. A few others maintained their own school, notably St. Leonard's at York, and in London after 1441 St. Anthony's—soon regarded as the best of London's schools. At Reading the decayed hospital of St. John the Baptist was used to house the local grammar school, a dependency of Reading Abbey; and at Lichfield the cathedral grammar school was endowed in association with St. John's hospital when the bishop refounded this c 1495—an early sixteenth-century master here was Robert Whittinton, an eminent grammarian and writer of school books. One of the best known schools in England at this time was attached to St. John's hospital at Banbury: its master John Stanbridge, another leading educationist, made Banbury celebrated for its progressive methods of Latin teaching.[14]

Winchester and Eton

The common feature of all these schools, however maintained, was their dependence on some ecclesiastical institution of one kind or other—a chapter, chantry, gild or hospital. It is the absence of this characteristic which makes the foundation of Winchester College in 1382 so important. 'For the first time,' writes Leach, 'a school was established as a sovereign and independent corporation existing by and for itself, self-centred and self-governed.'[15] Its founder, William of Wykeham, bishop of Winchester, was one of England's richest men, and his school reflected his wealth. It consisted of seventy 'poor and needy scholars' admitted from the age of eight upwards, living together and studying grammar, with a number of priest-fellows and choristers, all under a warden. The bishop's object was to prepare his scholars for promotion to New College, Oxford, where they became fellows after two probationary years. Very soon other boys were attracted to the school from far afield as 'commoners', and these lodged in the city, some being boarded in the Sisters' hospital.

Closely copying Winchester, Henry VI founded Eton College in 1440 when he was 18. After enlargement in 1443 this too consisted of a community of seventy 'poor and needy' grammar scholars admitted from 8 to 12 years of age, with fellows, chaplains and choristers, all living a common life under a provost. The scholars were

20

intended to pass to King's College, Cambridge, as Wyke-ham's passed to New College, Oxford. With its royal patronage and lavish endowments, Eton at once became the most celebrated school in England, attracting the sons of the nobility and gentry as 'non-foundationers', who lived in the town as 'oppidans'.[16] Thus Winchester and Eton were really the first public schools in the popular, present-day sense of the term.

Decay of grammar teaching

Notwithstanding the number of new school founda-tions in the fifteenth century, there were frequent com-plaints of the decay and disappearance of schools and of a consequent deterioration in grammar teaching. A Lon-don rector, William Byngham, declared in 1439 that the supply of clergy was being endangered by the lack of schoolmasters, and he claimed to know of seventy or more schools east of a line from Hampton to Coventry and north to Ripon that had become empty over the past fifty years because of the great scarcity of grammar masters. In 1447 a petition for four new schools in London presented to the Commons in parliament also drew attention to the declining numbers of grammar schools in the country and the harm that resulted.[17] In an endeavour to increase the supply of grammar masters William Byngham instituted God's-house at Cambridge in 1439, himself becoming its first head or proctor. His foundation was for 24 scholars or fellows who were to study grammar and other liberal arts, and were bound after graduating to accept any school appointment offered them at an adequate salary. The college pro-vided its own lectures, and they were continued during the long vacation so that schoolmasters could attend when their schools were closed for the harvest. God's-house has been called 'the first secondary-school training college', but analogies of this kind are apt to be misleading—obviously it bore little resemblance to a modern college or university department of education. Refounded as Christ's College by Lady Margaret Beaufort in 1505 it became like any other college, except that 6 of the 47 undergraduates then provided for had to take degrees in grammar and become schoolmasters.[18]

Another result of the decay of grammar teaching was that several fifteenth-century founders of colleges at the universities made provision for the teaching of grammar in preparation for the arts course. One of the most notable schools of the time was that established in connexion with Magdalen College Oxford, c 1478 by Bishop William Waynflete of Winchester, a former headmaster of Winchester and provost of Eton. The master and usher were to teach grammar not only to the younger members of the college but also to any other boys who presented themselves. Under its first master, John Anwykyll, and his usher and successor, John Stanbridge, later of Banbury, Magdalen College School became an influential centre of reformed Latin teaching by means of English, producing a number of prominent grammarians, among them Robert Whittinton and William Lily.[19]

Pre-Reformation schools

Early in the sixteenth century several other schools were endowed on much humbler lines than Winchester and Eton but like them existing in their own right independently of any ecclesiastical institution, but with some external body acting as governors. The ancient cathedral school of St. Paul's having decayed, a new one was established in 1509 by the dean, John Colet, and committed not to the dean and chapter but to the trusteeship of the London mercers' company. When Agnes Mellers founded Nottingham High School in 1513 (probably endowing an older school) it was the mayor and corporation that she made patrons and governors. Originally Manchester grammar school was the school of the collegiate church, later being endowed by a chantry foundation; Bishop Hugh Oldham further endowed it in 1515, but after reconstitution in 1525 the school was put under the control of a body of twelve laymen. To see in these arrangements any manifestation of pre-Reformation anti-clericalism would perhaps be unjustified, but they do show that the lay element in education was becoming increasingly important.

On the eve of the Reformation a school which was intended to be an autonomous college like Eton and Winchester was founded at Ipswich in 1525 by Cardinal Wolsey. It was to consist of a community of grammar scholars with chaplains and choristers, all ruled by a dean, and organically linked with Cardinal College at Oxford. Although the school did not survive Wolsey's fall, it is historically interesting because its statues, made in 1528, throw the first clear light on school organization and curriculum.[20]

Curriculum and method

For both these matters evidence before the sixteenth century is very thin indeed. Theoretically the grammar school taught the *trivium* but it was perhaps only the larger or more successful schools which taught much logic and rhetoric, so overlapping with the university as sixth forms do nowadays. Undoubtedly the staple was grammar—how to read, write and speak Latin. This was the basis of all formal education—'the foundation, gate and source of all the other liberal arts', says Wykeham's foundation deed for Winchester College.

The standard school grammar was by Donatus, a fourth-century Roman schoolmaster—whence a grammar-school boy was a 'donatist' or 'donat'; the standard grammar for reference was by Priscian, a fifth-century Byzantine; and the commonest readers were Aesop's *Fables* and the *Disticha* (moral maxims) of Dionysius Cato. All these were in universal use for over a thousand years—a testimony to the conservatism and veneration for authority which are striking features of mediaeval education. Mediaeval Latin has often been dismissed as 'dog Latin' or 'monkish Latin', but at least it was a language which met the practical needs of the time; and, however crude and graceless at its worst, it seldom fails, in official documents at any rate, to be grammatical and intelligible. Without direct evidence it is uncertain to what extent classical authors formed part of Latin teaching, but from fairly frequent quotations and allusions it is clear that some classical study must have gone on throughout the middle ages, though perhaps more for grammatical than for literary purposes.

About methods of teaching we know little. Books for school use must have been prohibitively expensive, and method relied on dictation and memory work. To aid rote-learning mnemonics were devised and books condensed into epitomes or written in metre. Donatus was usually learnt at school in a compendium, the *Ars minor*; more advanced, Priscian was abridged in the *Ars major*; and an intermediate grammar, the *Doctrinale* by Alexander de Villedieu, took the form of some three-thousand rhyming hexameters. Although ability to communicate in Latin was the great end of grammar, the master's exposition was in the vernacular, and for some two centuries after the Norman Conquest this was French; thus the educated clerk in England was more or less trilingual. The chronicler Ranulf Higden, a monk of Chester, observed c 1347 that French was still used for construing in English schools: two Oxford grammar masters, John Cornwall and Richard Pencrich were said in 1385 to have brought about the change from French to English in the mid-fourteenth century. How the vernacular was employed is uncertain, but the use of informal everyday English phrases (*vulgaria*) with Latin equivalents was the famous innovation of Magdalen College School, and grammars based on this method in early Tudor times were to oust Donatus and the *Doctrinale* from the schoolroom.

Besides Latin, religion no doubt played an important part in grammar-school routine, but perhaps less as a subject of instruction than through daily practice when founders and benefactors were commemorated. Nevertheless, the simple formularies of Catholic belief were evidently taught, and parsed and construed for thorough understanding. The bishop of Exeter complained in 1357 that these things were being neglected and he ordered the schoolmasters of his diocese not to put their pupils on to pagan books before they could parse and construe the *Pater Noster* and *Ave Maria*, the Creed, Matins and Hours of the Blessed Virgin Mary.[21]

Our first exact knowledge about the curriculum dates from 1528-30. Cardinal Wolsey, in his youth an usher at Magdalen College School, outlined the course of study for his school at Ipswich in 1528; and by a lucky chance the timetables of Eton and Winchester c 1530 also survive.[22] There were seven forms at Eton and Winchester, eight at Ipswich, and their time was devoted exclusively to Latin grammar, Latin authors, Latin composition and verse writing, with the addition in certain forms at Eton of the rules of good manners (from the recent book *Quos decet in mensa*), and the proper hymns. To generalize from this information about other schools and earlier periods would be dangerous, for no doubt much of the teaching would depend on the individual schoolmaster. Colet suggests an absence of detailed uniformity when, drafting his statutes for St. Paul's, he confesses that 'what shall be taught it passeth my wit to devise and determine in particular'.

Where mediaeval grammar-school boys learnt to write is another point of some obscurity. 'Writing throughout the middle ages,' Professor V. H. Galbraith tells us, 'was in general a matter for experts and a profession', and in the twelfth and thirteenth centuries a class of professional scribes (*dictatores*) came into existence, some of whom taught their art (*ars dictaminis*) as well as practising it. This comprised not only handwriting but literary and legal composition—private letters and the forms of official documents. In the fourteenth century professional writing-masters appear, some of them compiling manuals of specimen letters for all occasions, like the Oxford masters Thomas Sampson and William Kingsmill. No doubt in towns grammar boys learnt writing from such as these, but in country districts where professional scriveners were rare the schoolmaster himself would be obliged to teach it. And in towns some boys received a training in writing and business methods in the private schools of the scriveners as a more useful alternative to the grammar school. Later in the middle ages some chantry schools taught writing: one of the three chaplains of Acaster College was specifically required by the founder to teach all aspects of the scrivener's art, and one of the three at Jesus College Rotherham, writing and accounts.

Elementary and vernacular education

By this time there were other schools besides writing-schools supplementing on a lower level the more rigorous training offered by the grammar masters. Reading-schools taught boys to read Latin without teaching them to speak and write it. Although the books used were principally the primer (the layfolks' service-book) and the psalter, the purpose was evidently not entirely ecclesiastical, for there were reading-schools kept by town corporations which charged fees at a lower rate than in the grammar school. Almost certainly some reading-schools taught English as well as Latin, for during the fifteenth century there was a growing class of literate laymen, indicated by a mass of vernacular religious and secular literature in prose and verse, all presupposing the existence of a reading public. Indeed, one must conclude that the reading of English was becoming general in towns except perhaps among the poorest people.

About the extent and content of more elementary education very little is known. From pre-Conquest times parish priests were repeatedly enjoined by ecclesiastical authority to teach the young, but it was almost certainly not a regular day school that was intended. Archbishop Pecham in 1281 laid down a programme of basic religious instruction which every parish priest was to expound to his flock. It consisted of the fourteen articles of faith, the ten commandments, the two evangelical precepts of charity, the seven works of mercy, the seven deadly sins, the seven chief virtues and the seven sacraments; and this probably indicates the content of most children's elementary schooling.[23] More than this many parish priests would be incapable of giving, for they were often simple men of peasant stock and barely literate themselves.

Some town children received more systematic instruction in the song schools which, like grammar schools, were common ancillaries of cathedral and collegiate churches, and sometimes also of larger parish churches and some monasteries. The primary purpose of these schools was to teach boys the choral parts of the church services, but to do this some spelling and reading would be necessary, and without any doubt boys other than choristers attended. The educational value of learning to read the Latin liturgy without sufficient grammar to understand it is dubious, but when any grammar was attempted clashes with the grammar master, jealous for his monopoly, were likely to result.

In the later middle ages the commonest source of elementary instruction was probably the chantry priests. Some of these were specifically endowed to teach the parish children, but usually no more than the elements of religion, with perhaps the rudiments of literacy known as the A.B.C.s or 'abseyes'. It may be that some chantry grammar schools for lack of demand ceased to teach Latin and offered instead little more than the A.B.C.s and reading in addition to the usual amount of religious knowledge. But even when not required by their statutes to keep a school, many chantry chaplains probably taught the local children, either to eke out their stipends with small fees or simply to occupy their time. The convocation of Canterbury in

28

1529 ordered all parish clergy and chantry priests when not performing divine service to occupy themselves usefully, 'teaching boys the alphabet, reading, singing or grammar'.[24] How much of this elementary education there really was, and to what extent it affected the literacy of the great mass of English people as distinct from the urban middle class there is no means of knowing.

III

Oxford and Cambridge

Origins, early migrations, inchoate universities

The origins of England's two ancient universities are still imperfectly known. From the fifteenth century to the seventeenth erudite antiquaries traced the origins of Oxford and Cambridge into the remote British past. Oxford, they decided, had been founded by Greek scholars who had come to Britain with Brut the Trojan after the fall of Troy, though the existing university had really been created by King Alfred. Cambridge owed its beginning to the exiled Spanish prince Cantaber, but it was King Arthur who gave it its first charter. Not until the new antiquarianism of the seventeenth century were these quaint fables discredited, but even late in Victoria's reign there were educated men who believed that King Alfred founded Oxford.

Mediaeval Europe's three archetypal universities, Bologna, Paris and Oxford, were a spontaneous growth of the twelfth century, the age of the wandering scholar. Their pioneer English historian, Dean Hastings Rashdall, started the theory that Oxford really sprang from an exodus of English scholars from Paris in 1167 when Henry II stopped intercourse with France to bring pressure to bear on the exiled Becket; but this migration is no more than an hypothesis, and Oxford had already been a centre of education for perhaps half a century.[25] Several English cathedral schools, as we have seen, were attracting scholars from a wide area in the late twelfth century, and why Oxford and not Exeter or Salisbury or Lincoln should have developed into a *studium generale*—a centre of study inhabited by a *universitas*, or organized community of masters and students—is not at all clear; though it was an important road centre with a royal castle and two monasteries, and its bishop—a possible source of interference—was conveniently far removed at Lincoln.

The twelfth-century student was a rootless person, wandering from one *studium* to another, attracted by the reputation of some particular master: it was only as the century advanced that settled communities of masters and scholars formed themselves. But these were still impermanent bodies, lacking buildings and fixed property. Students lived where they could, and lectures were given in churches or hired rooms. At Oxford, university life revolved about the parish church of St. Mary the Virgin and the neighbouring streets and lanes. Migration was thus easy, and any dispute among scholars or between them and the town authorities might be followed by a dispersion, which could threaten the continued existence of a town as a *studium generale* and give rise to other universities. Indeed, many of the universities of mediaeval Europe were formed by migrations. Thus, in 1209 Oxford scholars dispersed in protest at the hanging of several of their fellows following a murder. Some of them went to Reading, where their colony was short-lived; others went to Cambridge, where the settlement proved permanent.[26] The fact that Cambridge should have become the seat of England's second university must be one of the accidents of history. An ancient river-crossing with a castle and a monastery, the town was nevertheless of only local importance, situated on the edge of the fens though conveniently near the thickly-populated region of East Anglia. Already by 1231, when it is mentioned for the first time, the university appears as an organized corporation of masters and scholars with its own chancellor.[27] Compared with Oxford, however, it remained of little account until the end of the fourteenth century, mainly dependent on the eastern counties, but certainly more than 'an obscure fenland seminary', which is how it was dismissed by the Oxford historian, H. A. L. Fisher. Perhaps much of the obscurity which envelops the early history of Cambridge results more from the destruction of its records during the peasants' revolt of 1381 than from its relative smallness and remoteness.

In 1238 Oxford was again dispersed, the scholars having been excommunicated after an assault on the papal legate. One group migrated to Northampton, later to be joined by others from Cambridge, and a nascent university here might well have become permanent had not Henry III suppressed it in 1265, partly to protect Oxford's interests, partly because the students had helped to defend the town against the king's forces during the late baronial rebellion.[28] Another group in 1238 went to Salisbury, where the cathedral was already a centre of learning, and the bishop in 1262 founded in the close a college of scholars (later De Vaux College) consisting of a warden and 20 fellows studying theology and the liberal arts which anticipated the colleges of Oxford and Cambridge and actually survived until 1542.[29] Here too, another university might easily have developed. The last serious migration from Oxford took place in

33

1333 when numerous discontented masters betook themselves to Stamford, where students had settled after the dispersal of the Northampton *studium* in 1265, and an incipient university here was terminated by Edward III at the supplication of the Oxford authorities in 1334.[30] Afraid of other secessions and another rival university, Oxford demanded of all candidates for the M.A. a special oath that they would never teach in Stamford, and—a measure of the conservatism of academic bodies—this continued to be taken until 1827.

Constitutional development

During the thirteenth century, although the danger of dispersion and migration remained, the age of the wandering scholar gave way to the age of settled academic corporations. Already by 1214 the *studium* at Oxford appears as a free community or university of masters and scholars with their own head, known then as *magister scolarum*, soon afterwards as chancellor. Their affairs are ordered by custom, not yet written down in the form of statutes, derived from the practices of the university of Paris. The curriculum and the administration of the university are based on the four faculties or major branches of study—Arts, Canon Law, Civil Law and theology. Only those who have completed the arts course and are masters of arts may teach in the schools (*scholae* = lecture rooms) or study in the higher faculties. Regent masters are those who reside in the university, lecturing to students in return for fees; non-regent masters are those who, having lectured for a period of years, have left the university for other employments though still remaining members of it. For their mutual advantage masters and scholars are org-

anized in imitation of the Paris system into 'nations',
though Oxford only has two, the river Nene apparently
marking the dividing line between 'northerners' and
'southerners'. Already by 1214 they have won certain
privileges in their contest with the townsmen, notably
immunity from lay courts and the right to have rents
and prices fixed by joint panels of masters and burgesses.

As the thirteenth century progressed the constitution
of the university took shape in a series of conflicts,
acquiring definite written form early in the fourteenth.
With the municipal authorities there was intermittent
warfare over such matters as the arrest and imprisonment of clerks, the fixing of rents and prices; and blood-
shed and homicide not infrequently resulted. The climax
was the tragic slaughter of clerks and pillaging of their
property on St. Scholastica's Day (10 February) 1355,
followed by the king's condign punishment of the town
and its virtual subjugation to the university, so that, as
Rashdall put it, 'the burghers lived henceforth in their
own town almost as the helots or subjects of a con-
quering people'.[31] With successive bishops of Lincoln
there was prolonged strife after 1280 over their demand,
in the cause of ecclesiastical discipline, to confirm the
university's nominee as chancellor; and this too ended
in eventual victory for the university after the intervention of the papacy. With the friars there was a long
struggle over their claim to take theology degrees without first passing through the arts course and also to have
the degrees conferred by the chancellor without reference to the faculty; but it was the friars who in the end
had to submit.

By the early fourteenth century, when custom had
hardened into statute, the chancellor, the head and chief
officer of the university, exercised wide judicial powers

over all its members, including the right to fine and imprison; and it was he who conferred the *licentia docendi*, by virtue of which alone a master could lecture in the schools. Executive authority in academic, financial and disciplinary matters also belonged to a number of annually-elected officers, the chief being the two proctors, all of whom were divided equally between the two 'nations'. All masters, regent and non-regent, sat in Convocation, the principal assembly of the university, which elected (and could remove) the chancellor, and made, amended and repealed statutes. To the regents assembled in Congregation belonged control of more routine matters and the election of the proctors and lesser officials. Voting was by faculty, the faculty of arts, as the most important, claiming a right of veto; and every master's vote counted equally. A broadly similar system of government, with control vested in the hands of all full members, developed at Cambridge. It was a democratic system, unlike the authoritarian regime of modern universities, where power tends to be concentrated in a senate of departmental heads.

Studies, lectures, disputations

The basis of all university studies was the faculty of arts, which in theory was devoted to the *quadrivum* —arithmetic, music, geometry, astronomy; the *trivium* being left to the grammar schools. From the mid-thirteenth century, however, the arts course consisted mainly of logic (which together with grammar underlay all university teaching method) and the three philosophies of Aristotle—moral, natural and metaphysical. Aristotle, made known in the West through Latin translations of Arabic versions of his works, received from the schoolmen a veneration scarcely less than that accorded to the Scriptures; to deny anything he had said was regarded as absurd; and he was not dethroned until the scientific renaissance of the seventeenth century. The full arts course, ending with the master's degree, took seven years and it was usually through this that a scholar approached one of the superior faculties— Civil Law, Canon Law, Medicine or Theology. Here the highest degree came to be that of doctor; originally the titles master, doctor and professor were used synonymously, master being the commonest, and the baccalaureate was only an inchoate or half-way degree. Theology represented the crown of university studies and the bachelor's degree in this faculty required seven years after the M.A., the doctor's two years more. For the bachelor's degree in civil law four years' study was demanded, five for the bachelor's degree in canon law, no additional time being specified for the doctorate.

Although grammar formed part of the arts course there was also a separate master's degree in grammar and a regular faculty or sub-faculty of the subject, but this was relatively unimportant and played no independent part in university government. The degree was a schoolmaster's degree, as the graduation ceremony indicates: a rod and 'palmer' were its insignia, and the graduand had to demonstrate his practical capacity by publicly flogging a 'shrewd boy', paying him 4d for his pains.[32] Degrees in music also appear in the fifteenth century, and unlike grammar degrees these have survived, though for long only on the fringe of university studies.

The lecture and the disputation together with the prescribed book formed the basis of all university teaching. Every student had to have his name on the roll

37

(*matricula*) of a master and attend his lectures. Although books were by no means rare, being hand-written they were expensive and students owned very few—an average bible in the thirteenth century must have cost about as much as the *Encyclopaedia Britannica* in the twentieth. Copies of prescribed texts were produced at the university's specification and sold or hired to students at fixed prices by the stationers, who employed parchment makers, scriveners, illuminators, binders— all important and privileged clients of the university. Each faculty had its set books and they were learnt almost by heart.

In the 'ordinary' lecture (*lectura* = reading) the master —speaking in Latin—systematically analysed and commented on the text and the standard glosses on it, his students committing his arguments to memory or writing them down. In the 'cursory' lecture he went over a book more rapidly and informally. Associated with the lecture were two different exercises—'repetitions', when the students repeated the arguments to one another to get them right; and 'questions', when the master or a student posed some problem (*questio*) to which reasoned replies ('responsions') in Latin syllogisms were given by other students, followed by the master's summing up or 'determination'. At intervals during the course there were more formal public exercises, again conducted in Latin, according to the strict rules of Aristotelian logic. The simplest of these was the 'question' on some particular point in a prepared text, to which the student made his 'responsions' in dialectical form, the master's 'determination' following. More difficult was the *quodlibet* ('whatever you please'), a proposition on any impromptu subject for extempore debate in Latin syllogisms at an open meeting held by the masters in Advent or Lent.

After four years of grammar, logic and rhetoric, the student performed his 'responsions' and then 'determined' other students' 'responsions', whereupon he was made a bachelor and allowed to assist in his master's school, giving 'cursory' lectures to supplement the master's 'ordinary' ones.[33] After three more years of Aristotelian philosophy he was allowed to 'incept' for the master's degree by performing in *quodlibets*, and so he became a full member of the university with the chancellor's licence to teach and able if he wished to continue his studies in one of the higher faculties. Thus, there was no hierarchy of salaried teaching grades as in the present-day university; every new M.A. was obliged to lecture as a 'necessary regent' for a period of one or two years—all he needed was a hired room to teach in, and pupils able to pay the fees which provided his livelihood. And in the deliberations of the university, as we have seen, one M.A.'s vote carried as much weight as another's.

University chests and buildings

Until the fourteenth century both universities possessed little but their rights and privileges. Their earliest property, the result of benefactions, consisted of chests of money from which loans were made to needy members under pledge, usually in the form of a book. The first of these at Oxford was established in 1240 and kept in the priory church of St. Frideswide, but the number steadily increased. Typical of them was the chest founded in 1306 by the executors of the bishop of Winchester: 40s was the limit for a regent master, 30s for a non-regent, 26s 8d for a bachelor, 13s 4d for other

MEA—D

students. Of buildings the universities had none: churches and hired rooms continued to serve for lectures, disputations and assemblies, and most students lived in ordinary houses, often in a group with their master. At Oxford *c* 1320 a congregation house and library were added to the north side of St. Mary's church, which long remained the hub of university life, but the Schools Quadrangle or lecture-room block was not built till the mid-fifteenth century, with an upper floor over the Divinity School to house the library given by Duke Humfrey of Gloucester after 1435. At Cambridge a schools quadrangle near Great St. Mary's church gradually took shape during the fifteenth century, aided by the generosity of Archbishop Thomas Rotherham. For their resources both universities were dependent entirely on the private benefactor; and the total income of Oxford university between 1464 and 1496 averaged no more than £58 a year—perhaps about £8,000 in modern money.

Halls and hostels

For students' residence the university as such made no provision. From the beginning students had boarded with townsmen or lived together in groups in hired rooms, but these 'chamberdeacons' were always a disorderly element and difficult to control. In the interests of discipline, and because students were often admitted as young as 13 and 14, it became more usual for them to live in licensed lodging houses, called halls or inns at Oxford, hostels at Cambridge, which were leased by masters at rents approved by the university. These halls were eventually brought under university supervision and the master or principal made responsible for his boarders' conduct, and partly for their academic instruction. Some 120 halls for grammarians, artists or legists are known to have existed at Oxford, though not all at one and the same time. They varied in size from a dozen to twenty or more students. Being unendowed many were shortlived, but in others an ordered life of study under successive principals went on for several centuries. For the better preservation of the peace, measures were taken in the fifteenth century to suppress the 'chamberdeacons' and compel all students to live in a hall under a master's supervision, or in private houses only with the chancellor's permission. Hence, as Professor Jacob points out, 'a modern university with its halls and its large body of students unattached to any foundation comes much nearer to the mediaeval pattern'.[34]

The early colleges

Into this pattern a new principle was introduced by the foundation of colleges. A college was an endowed, self-governing corporation of scholars living a common life of study, and in return for their founder's charity offering perpetual intercession for his soul. The founder was usually a wealthy ecclesiastic, often a bishop enriched in the king's service, and his purpose was to provide opportunities for a privileged minority of senior scholars to undertake the lengthy post-graduate courses in law or theology, so to increase the supply of highly qualified clerks for the service of Church and state. Being endowed and autonomous, colleges had a permanent existence quite independent of the university; at first they provided no teaching and their members (*socii* = companions or fellows) were few and select. Until the

41

sixteenth century the vast majority of graduates and undergraduates had no connexion with any college.

Although the first colleges—originally called halls—were founded in the later thirteenth century, their development is a characteristic of the fourteenth. University College and Balliol College at Oxford were the first to be endowed, but they did not at once achieve collegiate existence and the earliest to be properly constituted was Merton College, founded between 1262-64 by Walter de Merton, a former chancellor of Henry III, for a warden and 20 fellows, preferably the founder's kinsmen. This number was later increased to about forty and a subsidiary class of undergraduate students living out in the town was added, so that when other colleges came into existence Merton remained exceptionally large; and perhaps because of this it became for part of the fourteenth century the most celebrated house of learning in England, possessing a remarkable library.[35] At Cambridge the first college was founded in 1284 by Hugh de Balsham, bishop of Ely, becoming known as Peterhouse from the adjacent parish church of St. Peter without Trumpington Gate, which served it as a chapel. Its statutes were copied from Merton's and provided for a master and 14 scholars, who were to be at least bachelors on election and to proceed to M.A. and then study theology.[36]

Colleges on these lines, often with definite regional connexions, were established in remarkable numbers in the first half of the fourteenth century: at Oxford—Exeter (1314), Oriel (1324-26) and Queen's (1341); at Cambridge—King's Hall (c 1317), Michaelhouse (1324), Clare Hall (1326), Pembroke Hall (1347), Gonville Hall (1349), Trinity Hall (1350) and Corpus Christi (1352)—the last unique in owing its foundation to the joint effort

of two of the town gilds of Cambridge. All these were
for small numbers of graduate scholars or fellows studying for the M.A. or higher degrees in the faculties of law
or theology—a tiny aristocracy of students in the university as a whole. The six Oxford colleges existing in
1360 contained altogether, it has been estimated, no
more than 73 members. Most colleges at this stage possessed only temporary or improvised premises—ordinary houses with necessary additions, a neighbouring
church being used as a chapel. The earliest specially
designed collegiate buildings surviving at Oxford are
two sides of Merton's Mob Quadrangle (c 1304-7) and
at Cambridge the Old Court of Corpus Christi College
(c 1352-78): this is the oldest enclosed college-quad-
rangle, a plan common then in monasteries, almshouses
and manor houses but later regarded as peculiarly
characteristic of college architecture.

A landmark in college development came in 1379
with the foundation at Oxford of New College by William of Wykeham, bishop of Winchester, to help make
good the loss of educated clergy during the Black Death.
This was the first of these corporations to be called a
college, and it was important and influential for several
reasons—because of its connexion with the sister school
at Winchester, which alone fed it with scholars; because
it was primarily intended for undergraduates, though
these started as probationary fellows and were expected
later to continue in the higher faculties; because of its
unprecedented scale—a warden and 70 fellows with
chaplains and choristers; and lastly because of the size
and completeness of its buildings. Virtually finished in
1386, these were designed round a closed quadrangle to
supply all the needs of the society—a 'hugely dominant
chapel' backed by a hall with kitchen, buttery and

43

pantry; warden's lodgings; muniment tower, bursary and library; and along one side of the quadrangle two storeys of chambers, each chamber accommodating three or four fellows who slept in common but had separate enclosed studies within it. The most splendid of collegiate foundations so far, New College provided a model for future college founders.[37]

Wykeham's closest and most illustrious imitator was King Henry VI who founded King's College at Cambridge on similar lines in 1441, an event which must have greatly enhanced the reputation of the smaller university and helped to make it more comparable to Oxford. After enlargement in 1446 this became the most privileged and most richly endowed society in either university, with a provost and 70 fellows supplied by the grammar school of the sister college at Eton, and franchises which included exemption from the jurisdiction of the university chancellor and (as at New College) its members' right to take degrees without examination by the university. How and when this last extraordinary privilege arose is unknown, but it survived until the reforms of the mid-nineteenth century.[38]

Two colleges at Oxford obviously influenced by Wykeham's were All Souls (1438) and Magdalen (1448). The former, established by Henry Chichele, archbishop of Canterbury, was not only an academic college but also a war-memorial chantry for the English dead in the French wars. It provided for a warden and 40 fellows—16 of them lawyers, 24 either artists or theologians, all to be of at least three years standing in the university; and it is the only college which still retains the mediaeval pattern of an all-graduate society.'[39] Magdalen College was founded by another bishop of Winchester, William de Waynflete, a former don and headmaster who be-

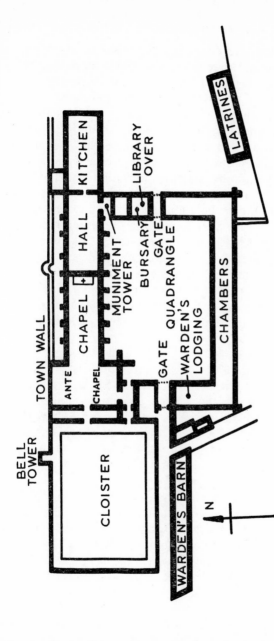

Fig. 1. New College, Oxford. Built mainly 1380–86: the architectural exemplar of the mediaeval academic college.

came Henry VI's chancellor. It consisted after 1480 of a president and 40 fellows, who were to be at least B.A.s and to take degrees in theology, law or medicine; but —a novel and noteworthy feature—it also provided for 30 undergraduate scholars ('demies') not less than 12 years old who were to study grammar until fit to start the arts course, and it was for these that a grammar school with master and usher was established within the college. Another striking innovation was the admission of a limited number of commoners (*commensales*), non-foundationers boarding at their own expense.[40]

Other colleges were founded in the fifteenth century but on a much less magnificent scale. Only one other was established at Oxford—Lincoln College (1427), expressly to train theologians to combat the errors of John Wyclif. Perhaps because of the lingering taint of heresy Oxford was now less favoured by patrons and benefactors than Cambridge, where four new colleges besides King's were started—God's-house (1439) to train grammar masters, as we have seen; Queens' (1448); St. Catharine's (1473); and Jesus (1496), the last consisting merely of six priest-fellows and some boys for whom a grammar school was attached. Excluding monastic colleges (for which see below pp. 58-59), in 1500 there were 12 colleges at Oxford, 13 at Cambridge; and on the eve of the Reformation Brasenose (1509) and Corpus Christi (1516) were added to those at Oxford, St. John's (1511) to those at Cambridge.

The last great pre-Reformation foundation, combining school and college in imitation of Wykeham's and Henry VI's, but intended to outshine both, was Cardinal Wolsey's at Ipswich and Oxford. Cardinal College, Oxford (1525), occupying the site of the dispossessed priory of St. Frideswide, was for a dean, 60 canons or fellows and 40 scholars, to be supplied by the school at Ipswich on the lines of Winchester and Eton. Wolsey's disgrace in 1530 came before his schemes had matured: his Oxford college was confiscated by Henry VIII and his Ipswich school was suppressed.

Because of the opportunities the mediaeval colleges afforded for advanced study and research, their educational contribution far exceeded their number and size. Nevertheless, because of their buildings and endowments it is easy to exaggerate their importance within the university as a whole. Dr. Salter, the historian of Oxford, believed that if every college had been abolished in 1400 the life of the university would have suffered no crushing blow. However, during the fifteenth century developments began to take place in the rôle of the colleges that were eventually to make them more important collectively than the university itself.

Students and their maintenance

What of the university students? Socially they were mainly of the middling ranks, sons of smaller landed families, officials, merchants, prosperous tradesmen, nephews or wards of ecclesiastics; but with a minority from either extremity of the social scale. A few were of noble birth, and rented entire inns or hostels for their companions and attendants. At King's Hall, Cambridge, established by Edward II and Edward III, the students were nominated by the Crown and came from the families of important royal servants and court officials.[41] Some, however, were of much humbler circumstances, but doubtfully of the servile class—though occasionally a villein might be manumitted by a generous lord in order to study. 'Poor and needy' (*pauperes et indigentes*)

47

is a phrase commonly used by mediaeval founders to describe their scholars, but it meant no more than students unable to manage without financial assistance, and these would be a majority in an age when degree courses might last half a lifetime and in an economy where ready money was always scarce.

How then were students maintained in an age when state aid was unknown? Most would be supported by parents or patrons, by allowances or legacies. Bequests for the 'exhibition' of sons or nephews are common in later mediaeval wills; usually they provide a specified annual sum for four years to the B.A. or, more seldom, for seven years to the M.A. Five marks (66s 8d) seems to have been an average, and Professor Jacob calculates that c 1450 a careful student in a hall could manage on 50s a year.[42] The poorest might act as personal servants to a regent master, or wait at table, or beg with the chancellor's licence; and any student possessing an appropriate pledge could meet a temporary emergency by borrowing from one of the university chests. The problem was most acute among aspirants for higher degrees. A favoured few of these would be college fellows, but they were perhaps never more than one in eight of the whole university population. The commonest form of financial support, particularly for advanced courses, was a canonry or a rectory, and with it a dispensation to be non-resident in order to study. But in an age without regular salaries, ecclesiastical preferment was the customary means of remunerating civil servants and other public officials, and a university crisis was caused by the great expansion of royal and ecclesiastical administration in the fourteenth and fifteenth centuries and the consequent scarcity of benefices for scholars. Periodically the universities submitted to the

Pope a consolidated list of their graduates who were seeking promotion to aid their studies, but this practice came to an end soon after 1390 when for political reasons appeals to Rome were prohibited. Hereafter, the university clerk had little hope of promotion from lay patrons, and royal and ecclesiastical patronage usually went to candidates for law degrees who supplied Church and state with their trained administrators.

This economic problem of student maintenance had profound effects on the universities. It contributed to a decline in student numbers—at Oxford from an estimated maximum of some 1,500 before the Black Death to no more than about 1,000 in 1438, though this may be less true of Cambridge, steadily growing in popularity in the fifteenth century. Poverty no doubt explains why perhaps as many as two-thirds of the students left without a degree, and why only a minority persisted as far as the M.A., a mere handful proceeding to the higher faculties. As a result there was an increase in graces exempting candidates from the statutory regulations prescribing periods of study and residence, and this led in time to the virtual disappearance of the higher faculties. No less important was the growing tendency of later college founders to provide for undergraduates and college teaching, for this was eventually to transform both universities.

Influence of the universities

Finally, what contribution did the mediaeval universities make to the society of their time and so, indirectly, to ours? Most of their learning, it must be admitted, is dead and completely forgotten, save by a few toiling mediaevalists; but by fertilizing the thought of successive

49

generations it prepared the way for modern science, for no advances in knowledge are independent of what has gone before. The training they supplied, it must also be said, had serious limitations by our standards: it was too exclusively intellectual, too dogmatic and disputatious: it ignored the imagination and the senses and produced men of capacious memory and mental subtlety who were nevertheless often vicious and uncouth. But however severely intellectual, the universities were never merely academic and theoretical—or rather they were academic and vocational, theoretical and practical at the same time. For the subjects they studied and the problems they discussed, though they may strike us now as remote and unreal, were intimately bound up with contemporary life and society. And most of the scholars who studied them did so less from any disinterested love of learning than from a desire to qualify themselves for promotion in the workaday world. From the thirteenth century the universities furnished the Church with its bishops, and the bishops with their judicial and administrative officials. From the fourteenth they supplied trained lawyers for the king's government in chancery and exchequer and diplomatic service. Church and state alike came to be administered by a bureaucracy of graduates, a development akin to the managerial and meritocratic revolution of our own time. And the crowds of students who left without degrees provided the country priests, the chaplains and schoolmasters, the clerks and secretaries of town corporations, gilds and manors. From the practical point of view, wrote Dr. Rashdall, the mediaeval universities' 'greatest service to mankind was simply this, that they placed the administration of human affairs—in short, the government of the world—in the hands of educated men'.[43]

IV

The monastic contribution

One aspect of mediaeval education that has been much discussed is the contribution made by monasticism. The once popular notion that somehow education in the middle ages was the work of monks was discredited half a century ago and no scholar would now admit the monks to have been a great educational force in later mediaeval England. Nevertheless, their exact rôle in education is still often misunderstood.

No doubt, as already suggested, most of such learning and formal education as there was in Anglo-Saxon times was to be found in monasteries, though there is no evidence of continuously existing schools, and when schools existed their influence can have touched very few people. However, with the twelfth-century renaissance bringing the secular cathedral schools and the embryo universities, and also a new monastic ideal which exalted the spiritual life rather than intellectual learning, monasticism ceased to play any significant part in the work of education. But its rôle did not cease altogether, and the problem is to discover how far the religious orders provided and promoted education of the laity between the later twelfth century and the Dissolution.

The religious orders

Before this matter can be properly considered something must be said, however briefly, about the various kinds of monks and the difference between monks and friars, for this will necessarily affect the discussion.[44] The original order of monks, and always the most influential and aristocratic, were the Benedictines or black monks, whose rule embodied the essentials of the monastic ideal: a common life of ordered worship, contemplation, and manual or intellectual work, in withdrawal from the world. Upon this ideal but with differences of emphasis, customs and dress, all the other orders were founded. First of these, introduced into England by the Normans, were the Cluniacs, a reformed offshoot of the Benedictines, laying particular stress on the liturgical life. Then in the great religious revival of the twelfth century came the Cistercians or white monks, seeking greater seclusion and emphasizing field work and manual labour; and the Carthusians who rejected the common life and devoted themselves to meditation and solitude. From the same religious renaissance sprang the various orders of regular canons, of which the Austin or black canons were the most widespread. These were at first different from monks in that they were priests combining the monastic life with parochial charges, though in later centuries canons and monks became almost indistinguishable. All these save the Carthusians had parallel orders of nuns, the Benedictine nuns having by far the largest number of houses. Quite distinct from all these were the friars or mendicants, of whom the two chief orders were the Dominicans (black friars or preachers) and the Franciscans (grey friars or minorities), both of which arrived in England in the 1220s. Whilst the monks worked out their own salvation in retirement from the world, the friars devoted themselves to the active work of popular evangelism: bound by the same monastic vows of poverty, chastity and obedience, they moved about the world living on alms, preaching, visiting and confessing. They represented the last great tide of religious revival in the middle ages and stole the popularity of the older monastic orders. Monks and friars reached their greatest numbers in the first half of the fourteenth century; thereafter the wastage was slow but continuous, and chantries and academic colleges became the more usual creations of the pious founder and benefactor.

Cloister schools

Until *c* 1150 monks were partly recruited from oblates —children dedicated to the cloister by their parents and brought up within the monastery, meanwhile—as boys—providing servers at mass and treble and alto voices for the choir. However, with the cessation of child oblation monasteries had to depend more for their recruits on postulants—young men who sought admission to the cloister from the outside world; and hence, suggests Professor Knowles, gradually developed the three kinds of schools sometimes provided by monasteries in the later middle ages.[45] In the cloister school the young monks and canons were taught the rule, the customs of the house, and sufficient Latin to enable them to take part in the services of choir and altar, sometimes by an older monk, but often by a paid secular, and usually in one of the cloister walks. Even in the largest monasteries the novices would seldom

53

exceed half a dozen, and smaller ones at times would have none at all. After Pope Benedict XII's reforms (1335-39) houses of Cistercians, Benedictines and Austin Canons were required by canon law to provide a grammar master for their novices but the evidence suggests that regular instruction in grammar was seldom available. Where it was, it affected very few, and those few isolated from the world, so that as far as the history of education is concerned the cloister schools are of little consequence.

Almonry schools

More important but still of uncertain extent were the almonry schools. These were kept by some monasteries as a charity for the poor boys of the neighbourhood, usually at the expense of the abbot or prior, and they were the general responsibility of the almoner, the monk-official in charge of almsgiving. They appeared in the early fourteenth century (at Ely in 1314), perhaps in response to the multiplication of private masses, which called for more altar servers, and to the new veneration of the Blessed Virgin Mary, which gave rise to Lady Chapels requiring a greater supply of singing boys; and in time no doubt some of these almonry clerks, but by no means all, would enter the cloister as postulants. The school was never taught by a monk but by a paid secular master, and it was usually held not within the monastery proper but near the almonry by the great gate. Song and reading with some grammar would be the staple of the teaching.[46]

Almonry schools, says Professor Knowles, were 'common if not ubiquitous among the black monks'; and they were often provided by Austin canons as well.

Because of their rural isolation the Cistercians made no contribution in this way, nor apparently did the Cluniacs and Carthusians, though foundations of these two orders were comparatively rare. By some houses, at some periods of time, the almonry boys were only boarded, being sent for education to a grammar school in the town. This was the practice, for instance, of the black monks at St. Albans, Tewkesbury and York, and of the Austin canons at Leicester. The Carthusians at Coventry and Hull also maintained 'poor scholars', and these almost certainly would attend a town school. In some houses—for example Ely in 1448 and Bristol in 1494—the same master taught the almonry boys and the young monks, but perhaps not both together.

Song schools

Later than the almonry schools and often associated with them were the song schools for training boys to assist with the chant maintained by many of the larger Benedictine abbeys. These were sometimes separate schools under a song master as at Glastonbury in 1534, when the abbot engaged a singing man to teach six children polyphony, and two of them to play on the organs; but in some houses the song boys seem to have boarded with the almonry clerks and to have shared the same master. At St. Peter's abbey in Gloucester in 1515, for reasons of convenience or economy, one and the same master was teaching grammar to the novices and 13 almonry boys, and song to five or six choristers.

Numbers in almonry and song schools are known only for particular houses at particular points in time.

In Reading in 1345 there were 10 almonry boys, in 1385 at Westminster 28, in 1520 at Norwich eight, at Durham 30 in 1535, at Thornton in Lincolnshire only two in 1440, though it was said there were usually 13 or 14. From such imperfect evidence it would be dangerous to attempt any but the roughest estimate of the total number of boys being educated thus at any period. In one place Leach suggested a total of 1,000 almonry children before the Dissolution, in another place his figure is 1,500;[47] and the discrepancy may suggest that he was merely guessing; probably that is all we shall ever be able to do. But set against a population of about three millions in 1500 the number of children educated free at the expense of monks and canons was obviously very small.

The abbot's boarders

In two other ways monasteries were associated with school education, though again without the monks themselves doing any teaching. Sometimes the sons of the nobility and gentry were taught the manners and accomplishments of their class in the castles and manor houses of great magnates. Equally they might be sent to be reared in the household of some abbot, living with him as his *commensales* or table-companions, doing him personal service but also paying him fees, and acquiring 'courtesy' from his steward and perhaps some book-learning from a chaplain or hired schoolmaster. This seems to have been common in establishments of Austin canons: living at Lilleshall abbey in Shropshire in 1534 were 'four gentlemen's sons and their schoolmaster'; and when the bishop of Norwich visited West Acre priory in 1494 he was told that there were many gentlemen's sons but the prior could not get the money for their board and tuition.

Monasteries as school governors

During the religious excitement of the twelfth century the new orders were the chief beneficiaries of pious donors. Some houses—Austin canons' notably—were then given estates on which schools happened already to exist, and in this way certain monasteries found themselves patrons or trustees of schools. Thus King Henry I gave property to the Austin canons of Huntingdon and Dunstable which in each case included the existing town school. So at this early period the school of Bedford passed to the neighbouring canons of Newnham priory, the school of Derby to the canons of nearby Darley abbey, and the school of Gloucester to the canons of Llanthony, just outside the town. The school at Reading was granted to Reading abbey soon after its foundation as a Cluniac house by Henry I; and schools at Lewes and Melton Mowbray later belonged to the Cluniac priory at Lewes.[48] In course of time some of these schools ceased to exist—apparently those at Bedford, Dunstable and Huntingdon, for instance; but others continued, though perhaps not without occasional intermissions, until the Dissolution. In these schools the master was appointed and possibly paid a salary by the abbot or prior or the responsible obedientiary; but he would be a secular clerk, perhaps even a married one, never a monk. The monk's vocation did not embrace teaching, and monks were not schoolmasters. *Monachus non docentis sed plangentis habet officium* says St. Jerome.[49]

Monks at the universities

To what extent was monasticism a force in higher education? To the twelfth-century renaissance some English monasteries had contributed significantly, notably in historical research and scientific studies. But in the thirteenth century, in both education and scholarship, they were entirely surpassed by the universities. Conscious of their eclipse, towards the end of the thirteenth century they started to send monks to Oxford. There in 1283 Gloucester College was established to accommodate student monks from Gloucester abbey, but soon afterwards it was opened to monks from other Benedictine houses. Each house contributed a room, so that the college was really a group of chambers each belonging to a separate monastery. About this time the cathedral priory of Durham started to send monks to Oxford; thus Durham College developed, being endowed in 1381 by Bishop Hatfield for eight monks and eight secular clerks acting as servants. Meanwhile the monks of Canterbury had provided a house of study which later lapsed, encouraging Archbishop Islip in 1361 to found Canterbury College for 12 students, both monks and secular servitors. At Cambridge a hall for monks from Ely was established in 1321, and after a century's intermission Buckingham College, a general house but controlled by Croyland abbey, followed in 1428. Other orders made much slighter provision for their members. As early as the 1280s the Cistercians had developed Rewley abbey in the suburbs of Oxford as a *studium*, but when it ceased to serve this purpose Cistercian student monks lived in private halls and lodgings like other scholars. Hence for their better accommodation St. Bernard's College was

58

started in 1437. The Austin canons may have lodged their students at the priories of their order, Oseney and St. Frideswide in Oxford, Barnwell outside Cambridge, until St. Mary's College was founded for them at Oxford in 1435.[50]

Thus, by the fourteenth century the sending of monks to study at the university had become a common practice, and it had been made a canonical obligation in 1336 by the Constitutions of Pope Benedict XII, which required one monk in every 20 to be sent to read theology or canon law. It is unlikely, however, that this rule was ever strictly obeyed. 'Had the Constitutions of Benedict XII been observed to the letter,' writes Professor Knowles, 'there would have been some two hundred monks, black and white, at the university at any given moment, and every abbey would have had about a quarter of its monks graduates. These figures were never attained, nor anything like them.'[51] Professor Jacob has estimated that c 1400, when the student population of Oxford was around 1,200, there might have been some 50 monks and from 10 to 40 canons. In the fifteenth century a few houses regularly sent students notably Canterbury and Durham to their own respective colleges; but outstanding monk-scholars were rare and bishops often found it necessary to complain of the ignorance of monks and their neglect of university study.[52] As late as 1513 Bishop Fox of Winchester planned a college at Oxford for monks of his cathedral priory but then changed his mind and founded Corpus Christi College for secular clerks instead in 1516. As Rashdall suggested, it was probably not so much love of learning that prompted monasteries to send an occasional scholar monk as their need for a competent theologian to preach or a canonist to attend to the legal affairs of the house.[53]

Monastic libraries

In one respect some monasteries had opportunities for study that were rare in the middle ages—they possessed, by the standards of the time, very large libraries. At Canterbury both Christ Church and St. Augustine's had immense treasures of books, so among others had Durham, Peterborough, Ramsey, Bury St. Edmunds, Reading and Glastonbury. They included not only bibles, service books, patristic theology and canon law but the standard works of the arts course and a wide range of Latin classics. Few of these seem to have been copied in the monasteries during the last century or so before the Dissolution, and the evidence suggests that perhaps not many of them were read. Although the monasteries had produced the great mediaeval historians there was none of note after Thomas Walsingham of St. Albans who died *c* 1422. The sometime Oxford university chancellor Thomas Gascoigne—admittedly a monk-hater—wrote in 1450, 'Formerly, learned books and valuable historical works were written in monasteries, but nowadays the religious allow their books to rot or to get lost; nothing can induce them to write new ones.'

Obviously, to generalize about the educational activities of over 600 monasteries over so long a period is rash, and there are bound to be exceptions. To confine ourselves to the century before the Reformation: Winchcombe abbey in Gloucestershire had an active cloister school for a time; an abbot of Peterborough, Edmund Kirton, founded a grammar school in his native Kirton-in-Holland; St. Albans had a celebrated biblio-

phile and classical scholar in Abbot John Whetamstede;
and the new humanism had its devotees among some
at least of the monks of Durham and Evesham.[54] But
these are exceptions, and the inescapable conclusion is
that during this period the monasteries counted for
little in education.

Nuns and the education of girls

From the monks we turn to the nuns. Their contribution to education is no more capable of statistical assessment than the monks', but relatively it was probably
greater, and may indeed have been their chief social
justification, even if not highly important. Professor
Eileen Power, still our authority on mediaeval English
nunneries, concluded that perhaps a majority of them
during the two and a half centuries before the Dissolution boarded and educated children, mainly girls but
often some small boys as well. Unlike the almonry and
song schools of the monasteries, these schools were
taught by the nuns themselves, and the children lived
within the convent, sleeping in the nuns' dormitory and
eating in their refectory—which is one reason why the
bishops disapproved of their school-keeping and tried to
limit it. For the nuns teaching was a financial expedient, not a work of charity, and only upper or middle-
class children who could pay the fees were received.
'So far as it is possible to be certain of anything for
which evidence is scanty,' Professor Power observes,
'we may be certain that poor or lower-class girls were
no more received in nunneries for education, than they
were received there as nuns.'[55] Other qualifications need
to be made about the educational activities of nunneries. The children they taught were not only socially

selected but numerically few. In 1440 at Stixwould in Lincolnshire there were 20 nuns and 18 children; in 1442 at Catesby in Northamptonshire 6 or 7 children and 7 nuns; at Winchester in 1536 there were 26 nuns and 26 girls, 'daughters of lords and gentlemen'. With sometimes 30 to 40 'gentlemen's children' Polesworth in Warwickshire seems to have been quite exceptional. Usually only two or three are reported, and ten would seem a generous average. If we accept Dr. Power's estimate that two-thirds of the nunneries may have admitted children we have a total of 900 or 1,000 out of a population of some three millions in 1500. Obviously the training they received would depend on the nuns' own educational standards, and these do not seem to have been very high. Ability to read, but not to write, English; perhaps some French, but rarely Latin; skill with the needle, some knowledge of herbs and samples —the ordinary attainments of ladies of good family outside the cloister : these were the usual accomplishments of nuns. Accordingly, the girls they taught probably learned little more than the elements of religion, English reading, needlework and good manners—the social refinements expected of gentlewomen.

The friars and higher education

Lastly, what of the friars? With the ordinary schooling of children they had no concern whatever at any period, but in higher education they were for a time the greatest force of all. The Dominicans from their inception regarded themselves as a student order with an intellectual vocation—every one of their convents was a school of theology or 'arts', and in their devotion to study they were quickly followed by the Franciscans, whose original ideal had been quite different, and later by the two smaller orders of Carmelite and Austin friars. The friars developed a self-contained system of scholastic training in their own houses for the education of their novices, certain convents being set apart for advanced theological study. The whole system was integrated with the universities through the general houses of study which the several orders maintained there. Thus a steady flow of trained lecturers and preachers was assured for the priories of each order. The apex of each system was its *studium* at the university, and it was here that the friars made their great impact. Dominicans and Franciscans were established in Oxford by 1224, at Cambridge soon afterwards, and Austin and Carmelite friars followed later. Within a few years the Franciscans made their Oxford convent 'the most brilliant centre of intellectual life in the country, a position which it continued to hold for more than a century'.[56] Their greatest masters, Roger Bacon, William Ockham and Duns Scotus, not only dominated the Oxford schools but also shaped the course of mediaeval thought. It was the Franciscans too who after *c* 1250 first gave Cambridge a place on the academic map. Apart from their influence on scholasticism the mendicants made important contributions to Middle English religious verse, and some were keen students of classical literature and antiquity, thus marking an important preliminary stage towards the Renaissance.

However, the friars' influence on university education was not only intellectual. Their permanent buildings and residential societies represented something new in university life and perhaps suggested the idea of the college. They provided the chief link with foreign universities. And their quarrel with the university over

63

their claim to take theological degrees without first going through the arts course prompted the authorities at Oxford to set down their statutes and privileges in writing for the first time. As the fourteenth century advanced the friars gradually lost their intellectual and academic pre-eminence, perhaps as new college foundations increased the number of secular masters. In the hundred years before the Reformation, with few exceptions, they were more notable for their preaching than their scholarship.

V

The reformation and English education

The Protestant revolt against late-mediaeval Catholicism

Until the 1530s all Englishmen were Catholics, their Church an organic part of a united Christendom ruled by the Pope. From childhood they were familiar with the miracle of the mass, prayers for the dead, the invocation of saints; and monks, nuns and friars were a normal feature of the daily scene. Then, within the space of thirty years or so, England became a Protestant country and Catholicism was proscribed. How did these changes come about and how was education affected by them?

Demand for reform in the Church was widespread in many parts of Europe in the early years of the sixteenth century among laymen and churchmen alike. Although personal and corporate devotion remained strong, the Church as an institution stood open to attack. Enormously wealthy and powerful, with its own courts and canon law and acknowledging the Pope as its spiritual and temporal head, it obstructed the sovereign nation states that were now emerging as a result of increasing royal authority and more efficient government machinery. Moreover, incongruity between the teaching and

65

practice of the Church was everywhere to be seen. The Pope was a worldly Italian prince in whom it was difficult to discern the Vicar of Christ. Bishops and higher clergy were lawyers and administrators appointed for loyal service to the king's government, not for their piety and sanctity; Cardinal Wolsey, the wealthiest pluralist of the age, who loaded his natural son with ecclesiastical preferments whilst still a schoolboy, was the supreme example of the political prelate in England. Parish priests were usually ill-educated, and morally no better than ordinary men. Monks and friars often failed to live according to their Rule. And among simple, uneducated people Catholicism had accumulated superstitious and materialist accretions—miracles, shrines, prophesies and relics, which the Church was almost powerless to control; whilst to the learned the primitive faith of the gospels had become obscured by the elaborate superstructure of scholastic theology no less than by these ignorant peasant cults.

Connected with the demand for reformation, but in ways not easy to define, was the Renaissance—the refructifying of art, literature and learning through the stimulus of the rediscovery of classical antiquity, which marks the later fifteenth and sixteenth centuries. Educationally, the Renaissance expressed itself in humanism, which meant a new interest in man and human perfectibility, the rejection of scholasticism, a passion for pure Latinity and the study of Greek; and with this went an increasing output of relatively cheap books of all kinds made possible by the invention of printing. Most influential of the northern humanists was the Dutchman Erasmus (d. 1536), who visited England several times and taught for two years at Cambridge. A prolific writer of schoolbooks, he was the principal means of introducing the cultivation of pure classical Latin into the schools. Although always a Catholic himself, he satirized with wit and elegance clergy, monks, friars, bishops and popes, the crabbed syllogisms of the schoolmen, the obscurantism and materialism of contemporary religion; and the newly literate, urban middle classes provided ready readers for his books, which the printing presses poured out. Among some scholars, including a small group at Cambridge in the 1520s, his Latin version of the New Testament helped to sow the intellectual seeds of Reformation.

State religion and the Church of England

In England the Reformation began with Henry VIII's desire for a divorce, and it took shape with his determination to sever the legal ties with Rome when Wolsey failed to obtain him a divorce from the Pope. The first stage, from 1529 to 1534, was predominantly political; it ended with the rejection of papal jurisdiction and the substitution of the royal supremacy over the Church in England: a revolution made easy by popular anti-papal feeling and the spread of reformist ideas from Luther's Germany. This was followed, for financial rather than religious reasons, by the dissolution of the monasteries, beginning with the smaller ones in 1536 and culminating in total suppression in 1539-40. This was a stupendous act of nationalization, and the disposal of monastic lands in the greatest property sale in our history was followed by the rise of the gentry to power as the English ruling class. More omnipresent and familiar than the monasteries, however, were the colleges of priests, chantries and gilds, and their dissolution and expropriation by Edward VI in 1548 was, so

67

far as ordinary people were concerned, an even more decisive breach with the Catholic past. The final stage was the reformation of doctrine; deeply influenced by Calvinism, this started under Edward VI and, after the brief Catholic reaction of Mary's reign, was accomplished in the early years of Elizabeth's. The Church of England that emerged preserved intact its ancient episcopal organization and legal structure, but had a new liturgy embracing Catholic and Protestant elements, set out in English in the Prayer Book; and a broad compromise theology summarized in the Thirty-nine articles. In 1559 the Queen was made its 'Supreme Governor' by the Supremacy Act; and by the Uniformity Act of the same year all her subjects were obliged under penalty to accept its form of worship and none other. During the greater part of Elizabeth's reign the overriding concern of the central government was to strengthen this new religious establishment, and protect it from dissentient minorities—Catholics on the one hand, and, to a less extent, radical Calvinist nonconformists on the other.[57]

The Reformation and education in England

The English Reformation was thus a thoroughly revolutionary movement, but one smoothly and peacefully carried out. It affected not only the religious beliefs and practice of English people, but also the constitution, the social life and economic structure of the country, reacting in ways which cannot be defined precisely with other developments that were simultaneously changing society. A fast growing population and consequent inflation were the concomitants of Reformation, and in their effects on education were

68

perhaps in the long run of even greater significance. The decline in the territorial power of the Church was also accompanied by the rise of a new class of landed gentry, many of them with a stake in former monastic and chantry estates, who came to control policy and government as Members of Parliament and justices of the peace. For this rôle they needed education, and hence they gradually invaded both grammar schools and universities, so tending to change the traditional complexion of both. Although the Church and clergy long remained important pillars of the English social order, in general the Reformation tended to be followed by a shift in emphasis from the theological and clerical to the secular and lay. And if in education and intellectual life the Church and religion continued to be powerful influences, their control was less complete than previously.

'In England from the first,' says Leach, 'education was the creature of religion, the school was an adjunct of the church, and the schoolmaster was an ecclesiastical officer.'[58] This being so, education was inevitably influenced by the Reformation. The question we now have to consider is in what ways it was affected, to what extent, and with what results.

I. THE SUPPLY OF SCHOOLS

Effects of the dissolution of the monasteries

First, what effect had the Reformation on the number of schools and the availability of education? Victorian scholars tended to see the monasteries as the only source of mediaeval education, for the population at large no less than for their own members. To Catholics, accepting the monks as the educators of an age of faith,

69

the destruction of the monasteries by Henry VIII was a disaster for England and the Old Religion. On the other hand, Protestants imagined pre-Reformation England submerged in ignorance and superstition, with no more than a few 'monkish' schools: enlightenment came when Henry VIII suppressed the monasteries and the boy King Edward VI gave England its ancient grammar schools, still known by his name.

These crude notions were overturned by Leach. His case was that the monks had really little to do with education, but that an abundant supply of schools for the needs of the population was provided by the churches of canons and the chantries, and that far from being a champion of schools Edward VI despoiled an existing educational system when he destroyed these foundations. To Leach the Reformation *was* a disaster, but it fell in Edward VI's reign, not Henry VIII's. This theory is now in its turn being discarded by historians who deny that there ever was a system of schools for Edward VI to destroy. 'The old legend of Edward VI as the patron of schooling is now dead,' wrote Dr. G. R. Elton in 1955, 'though the newer legend of the great system of education available in the old chantry schools still awaits overthrow.' Since then Professor W. K. Jordan of Harvard has attempted to discredit the whole mediaeval legacy of schools and argues that our secondary-school system really dates from a profusion of grammar schools founded in late Tudor and early Stuart times. The most recent assessment of these changes, by Mrs. Joan Simon, marshals all the evidence amassed since Leach's time and examines it in the light of the social forces of the age, advancing a much more balanced and acceptable conclusion.[59]

Between 1536 and 1540 some 500 houses of monks and canons were dissolved by Henry VIII. To make an accurate estimate of the consequent loss to education is impossible because we are ignorant about so much that is relevant—how many houses actually maintained almonry and song schools, how regularly they were kept, how many pupils they had and what proportion of them were non-clerical, at what level they were taught, and so on. Nevertheless, there must have been some loss. The opportunities for upper-class boarding education were reduced. An indeterminate number of almonry schools came to an end, but with a total loss no greater perhaps than two or three present-day secondary schools. On the other hand, it seems that most of the schools under the governance of monasteries survived the Dissolution, receiving an endowment out of Crown lands and eventually new trustees, though sometimes not without a short break in continuity.

As a direct result of the Dissolution several other schools were established, or re-established on a more permanent basis, and still exist. By an Act of 1540 all eight monastic cathedrals were reconstituted as secular foundations like York or Lincoln or Salisbury, having a dean and chapter of canons instead of a prior and convent of monks. In each of these 'cathedrals of the new foundation' a grammar school was made an integral part of the establishment under the dean and chapter; and Henry VIII's statutes prescribed in detail the appointment and duties of master and usher, the number of foundation scholars, the curriculum, organization and conduct of the school and so on. Thus there came into being the King's Schools at Canterbury, Ely, Rochester and Worcester, and, in a new form, the grammar schools at Carlisle and Durham. Educationally if not legally they were a continuation of the bishops' old-established city schools, and they may also have incorporated the almonry and novices' schools as well. For instance, at Canterbury the master of the archbishop's school in the city became the first headmaster of the King's School, and of the first 50 King's Scholars nine were ex-novices or junior monks of the cathedral priory.[60] At Durham the first headmaster of the new cathedral school was the last master of Bishop Langley's school, and he continued to use the dwelling house and schoolroom of Langley's foundation. On the other hand the King's School at Worcester was entirely new, and the old bishop's city school, long supported by the Trinity gild, was separately refounded as the Free School with six 'discreet citizens' as governors: it is now the Worcester Royal Grammar School. At Norwich a King's School sponsored by the new chapter was unnecessary because the old city grammar school of the bishops was refounded by the city corporation, forming the present Norwich School. Winchester cathedral was exempted from the scheme because of the existence of Winchester College.

In addition to these reconstituted cathedrals, six of the greater dissolved abbeys—Bristol, Chester, Gloucester, Oxford, Peterborough and Westminster—were elevated to cathedral rank in 1540-42, serving new dioceses. With the exception of Oxford, which was already well provided for by Magdalen College School, the chapters of all these new cathedrals were each required by their statutes to establish a grammar school. So were created the present King's Schools at Chester, Gloucester and Peterborough and the Cathedral School at Bristol. The school at Westminster carried on the traditions of the old almonry school, and was eventually refounded as part of the establishment of the collegiate church of Westminster Abbey by Queen Elizabeth in 1560.[61]

Being thus securely established and in relatively populous and important towns, these ranked among the leading schools of the country until the emergence of the 'public' schools at the end of the eighteenth century; and Westminster in the seventeenth and eighteenth centuries rivalled both Eton and Winchester. It might be argued therefore that on balance schooling gained rather than lost through the Dissolution. 'Far more indeed should have been made of this unique opportunity,' comments Professor Dickens, 'but the share which went to education cannot justly be called insignificant.'[62] Plainly it is inconsistent with the facts to claim, as another recent historian of these events does, 'that education came away empty handed from the whole proceeding'.[63]

If school education suffered damage it was more likely to have been from the passing of the nuns. One may perhaps assume that of the suppressed nunneries some seventy or eighty had boarded girls, and there is some evidence that this service had been appreciated by the gentry. But whilst the loss of educational facilities for several hundred upper-class girls must be added to the reckoning, obviously it cannot be regarded as a national disaster.

One other educational consequence of the Dissolution must be briefly noted here. With the end of the monasteries came the end of their houses of study at the universities. This certainly caused no great damage to university education for, as we have seen, the monks played little part in university affairs; also as

73

we shall see later (p. 97), their college buildings were all very soon put back to academic use.

Effects of the dissolution of the chantries

If the fall of the monasteries brought no educational catastrophe, what of the later suppression of the colleges of priests, chantries and gilds? An Act of 1545 conferred these on Henry VIII personally, with the declared object of raising funds for national defence; but he died before suppression had made much headway. Another Act in 1547 granted them to the young Edward VI, and—the reforming protestant party now being in the ascendant—the alleged purpose of confiscation this time was to put down popish superstition, especially the 'vain opinions' about purgatory and masses for the dead perpetuated by the chantries, and to endow education on the proceeds. County commissioners were appointed to survey and report on all these foundations, and as from Easter 1548 all collegiate churches, chantries and gilds with a few named exceptions were to be dissolved and expropriated. But a school existing as an integral part of any one of these foundations was to be spared, the property 'to remain and continue in succession to a schoolmaster . . . forever . . . for . . . the keeping of a grammar school'.[64] The Commons passed this measure unwillingly: towns were naturally reluctant to risk losing the educational and other charitable services which some of these religious institutions afforded, and there was some opposition led by the burgesses for King's Lynn and Coventry. The resistance might have been sterner if it had been known that the Act was not to be observed in the letter, for in July 1548 two royal commissioners were

74

appointed to recommend which schools should be continued, not however with a grant of the property, but with an annual Crown stipend equal to the net income of the property at the time of suppression.

The truth about the 'Edwardian spoilation' of education, as Leach called it, is impossible to appraise statistically. According to the traditional calculation 2,374 chantries and chapels and 90 colleges came to an end in 1548 and their property was nationalized. But we do not know how many of these foundations actually then supported schools, statutorily or voluntarily. From the admittedly incomplete records of the 1545 survey and the much fuller ones of 1547 Leach counted 259 chantry schools, but these he believed were not all that existed. His 'modest estimate' was 300 grammar schools 'most of them . . . swept away . . . or, if not swept away, plundered and damaged'.[65]

A serious weakness in Leach's case is his assumption of continuity. He takes it for granted that a school mentioned two or three times in as many centuries existed uninterruptedly in between and so to the Reformation. This is a rash supposition, and also an astonishing one in view of Leach's own experience of late nineteenth-century conditions, when many small grammar schools decayed and died. In the fifteenth century, as we have seen, there were numerous complaints of the disappearance of schools and consequent decay of grammar teaching; and although detailed instances of Byngham's allegation have not been collected, it seems probable that many late mediaeval schools existed intermittently and in some cases vanished altogether through neglect or abuse or poverty —as many hospitals and other charitable and religious institutions undoubtedly did.[66] Certainly this would help to explain the low educational standards of many of the poorer country clergy on the eve of the Reformation, for which there is abundant contemporary evidence.

Not only is there doubt about the permanence of schools, but it is likely that many of those founded as grammar schools had ceased in time to teach Latin through lack of demand and became humble A.B.C. schools, just as some rural grammar schools became elementary schools in the nineteenth century. For the same reason schools in remote and sparsely populated areas must have been very small, no more than a dozen or a score of boys. Numbers of pupils are seldom mentioned in the chantry returns, but where they are they are probably the exceptionally large ones—for instance 120 at Skipton, 104 at Lancaster, 100 at Worcester; the inhabitants, anxious to preserve their school, would have good reason to quote figures like these, and perhaps even to inflate them.

These considerations suggest that we ought not to overrate the amount of schooling available before the Reformation, as Leach does. On the other hand there must have been considerable private or unendowed teaching of which we have no record and which it is quite impossible to gauge. Archbishop Thomas Rotherham expressed gratitude in his will to the grammar master who chanced to come to Rotherham when he was a boy there (in the 1430s), and whose teaching enabled him and others to rise to greater things; and there must have been much adventitious teaching of this kind. Some no doubt was provided by better educated curates, and by chantry priests who were not bound by their statutes to teach; right up to the time of their suppression chantry priests were being commanded by their bishops to 'exercise themselves in teaching youth to read and write', and the canons of Canterbury convocation in 1529 had included grammar as well.

However, it is clear that there was some public disquiet about the harm done to schools in the two or three years following the Chantries Act. This was caused by the rapid sale of chantry lands to private purchasers and the diversion of the proceeds from education to easing the government's pressing financial difficulties—because of the economic situation some schools which might have been preserved were not, and there was delay in the payment of Crown stipends to some masters of schools whose continuation had been authorized. Nevertheless, most of the schools covered by the Act (that is, those legally part of a foundation) were continued by warrants issued as early as July and August 1548, and the Crown stipend awarded to the master, being equal to the current net value of the whole endowment, often exceeded the salary he had previously received. For instance, Bishop Alcock's chantry schoolmaster at Hull had received an annual salary of £10, but his Crown stipend after 1548 was £13 2s. 2¾d. After some early arrears during the government's years of near bankruptcy these allowances were paid with fair regularity. But being fixed they steadily depreciated with the mounting inflation that had lately started, and before long these schools suffered crippling poverty.

Some of them, however, were soon put on a stronger footing by the action of the local inhabitants, anxious to safeguard their school. For example, that at Skipton, continued on a stipend of only £4 4s., was immediately further endowed by William Ermysted, a local man risen through government service, who committed the patronage to the vicar and churchwardens. Similarly, the school at Lichfield, continued with small fixed stipends for a master and usher, was shortly afterwards re-endowed by the bishop's steward. And after 1551, when the government's worst crisis had passed, several towns successfully petitioned for the refoundation of the local school under municipal trusteeship with a grant of former church lands. These are the so-called King Edward VI grammar schools, a few refounded by Act of Parliament, others by letters patent. Thus, the school at Retford, continued in 1548, was re-established in 1552 under the bailiff and burgesses, who drew up statutes for it in consultation with Archbishop Holgate. At Louth, as at Stratford-on-Avon, the town had no independent corporate existence until it was given a charter in 1552 in order to govern the local restored school, so that the school governors really became the municipal authority. Elsewhere, rather than lose a valuable asset to the community, a town corporation would gradually assume responsibility for the local school without a charter having been sought, the corporation supplementing the master's government stipend out of the borough fund, as at Hull, Lancaster and King's Lynn.

Unfortunately, schools that were incidental, and not statutory, parts of any of the religious foundations covered by the Act did not receive continuation warrants; but some of them survived, notwithstanding. This was so in the case of several schools formerly provided by collegiate churches, where education had never been explicitly endowed but maintained by custom out of the common fund. A number of these churches were expropriated late in Henry VIII's reign, and their schools in some cases disappeared. However, when St. Mary's Warwick was dissolved in 1544 the townspeople secured a grant of the school which the college had maintained, and it was re-founded with the town incorporated as governors. Under the Act of 1547 the chapter at Ripon was abolished and with it its school, but after a local petition to the Crown a new school was founded by royal charter in 1554, the governing body consisting of 'eight or ten of the best disposed, discreet and most substantial of the town and parish'. At Beverley likewise the school died with the chapter, never having been specifically endowed; and in 1552 the burgesses appealed to the Crown for a grant of some of the recently confiscated estates of the minster, pleading that the town had a population of 5,000 and now no school. But their plea was unsuccessful, and the town corporation perforce soon assumed control of the school which the canons had maintained for over four centuries. In some other places it would appear that schools of this kind survived or were soon restored with local support, even though denied continuation warrants and government stipends.

Of course, many schools were unaffected by the Chantries Act. Specifically excluded were the colleges at Eton, Winchester, Oxford and Cambridge, and all cathedral chapters; and the schools associated with these bodies went on as before. In the period before the Reformation a few schools of the old secular cathedrals had benefited from endowments—for example, at Chichester by a unique arrangement a prebend was appropriated to the schoolmaster in 1497; but others seem to have existed in some obscurity. From this they emerged, after Edward VI's injunctions in 1547 had ordered every cathedral without a grammar school to establish one, with a master at £13 6s. 8d. a year and an usher at £6 13s. 4d., both paid out of the common fund. Generally, these schools were now transferred from the chancellor's control to that of the dean and chapter as a whole. Thus, St. Peter's at York came to be endowed and re-housed in 1557. At Lincoln the chancellor's grammar school down in the city had long suffered competition from a second one, established in the close and allowed by the chapter for the choristers' convenience; eventually, after protracted discussions, the two were united in the former Franciscan friary in the city, the dean and chapter agreeing to appoint and pay the master whilst the corporation accepted responsibility for an usher and for schoolroom repairs. In Elizabeth's reign the cathedral schools at Exeter, Hereford and Wells were reconstituted under the dean and chapter; but at Salisbury a new school was placed under the city corporation.

Also untouched by the Edwardian dissolutions were, of course, those schools which existed independently of any religious foundation, being under the trusteeship of town corporations, like Bristol and Nottingham, or having their own governing bodies, like Manchester grammar school and the Crypt School at Gloucester—to name only a few. Moreover, as a beneficial by-product of the dissolutions, it seems quite likely that the numbers of private-venture teachers would be swollen for a time at least by dispossessed and unpensioned chantry priests, driven to keep schools in order to make a living.

Thus, in the absence of definitive evidence it appears reasonable to suppose that at most Edward VI's action caused some brief dislocation of schools, but no wholesale closures. Admittedly, the award of fixed stipends soon injured many schools, though the government cannot fairly be blamed for that. Most chantry schoolmasters had received fixed salaries, and subsequent school founders provided salaries at current rates which took no account of price rises. And once ex-chantry property had been sold to ward off bankruptcy, it is difficult to see what could have been done to repair the damage by a government living from hand to mouth in an inflationary economy.

New grammar schools and their founders

To assess the importance of these events as they affected school provision they must be seen in perspective, and then there is much to be said for Professor Jordan's view that 'the whole discussion of this question so exclusively in terms of the Reformation seems at once unfortunate and a little irrelevant'.[67] Taking ten sample counties, including London, containing altogether about a third of the country's population, he analysed the amounts bestowed on social good works, including schools and universities, between 1480 and 1660. The foundation of grammar schools, he shows, went on at varying rates of increase throughout this period, but was especially rapid between 1550 and 1640, when private charity produced an enormous expansion of grammar-school education. This was by no means a new revelation, but the statistical evidence had certainly never before been so elaborately assembled. The chief weakness in his argument arises from his failure to adjust his figures of bequests and donations to the changes in monetary values over this notoriously inflationary period. Thus adjusted, his figures might suggest that the greatest expansion actu-

81

ally took place in the last generation of Catholic England.[68] Jordan's disparagement of late mediaeval education, springing partly from incomplete knowledge of local examples, is also much too sweeping: he underrates the amount of pre-Reformation schooling as Leach overrates it. His main thesis, however, must be accepted: an increase in schools went on throughout the Tudor period and the dissolution of monasteries and chantries had no appreciable effect on the general trend.

Who were the people who gave their money to found or endow these grammar schools in such a flood of generosity after the mid-century? According to Jordan's analysis all social classes contributed, but principally the gentry, the clergy, and most of all the merchants. Their motives no doubt differed. Country gentlemen were now no longer content to rely on the literacy of a secretary or chaplain. Influenced by the new humanist ideal of the cultivated man of affairs serving the state—*il cortegiano* of Renaissance Italy— they now patronized the grammar schools, seeking a liberal education preparatory to the university and the Inns of Court, partly for personal culture, partly to fit themselves for service in Parliament and Quarter Sessions. To the traditional upper-class training in arms and physical skills there now had to be added more urbane and intellectual accomplishments; and this new ideal of the gentleman powerfully affected education in later centuries. On the other hand, Elizabethan churchmen, especially the bishops—who were almost as outstanding among school founders as their mediaeval predecessors—wanted a more educated clergy to defend the Church of England. How necessary this was is shown by Bishop Hooper's visitation of Gloucester diocese in 1551—out of 311 clergymen questioned, 170 could not repeat the Ten Commandments, 10 could not say the Lord's Prayer, and some did not even know who was its author. Meanwhile, the merchants of Elizabeth's reign, many of them Puritans risen to wealth from poverty, wanted schools to help fashion a society wherein careers would be open to talent, as well as to train up a godly preaching ministry to spread the gospel and advance protestantism throughout the kingdom. For them ignorance, begetter of both poverty and popery, was the enemy whom the grammar schools were founded to combat. But behind these varied and not always disinterested motives were the pressures of a rapidly rising population—a rise not yet accurately investigated or explained, but perhaps as much as 40 per cent between 1500 and 1600 and 30 per cent between 1600 and 1630. As Professor W. G. Hoskins observes, 'Elizabethan England suddenly filled up with children', especially after the 1560s,[69] and this alone would make more schools urgently necessary.

Every region furnishes examples of schools founded by these different groups of benefactors at this time. For instance, in Elizabeth's reign the Derbyshire gentry endowed grammar schools at Chesterfield, Wirksworth, Dronfield, Ashbourne and Risley. Among ecclesiastical founders Archbishop Parker established Rochdale grammar school; Archbishop Sandys, Hawkshead; Bishop Pilkington, Rivington; Dean Nowell of St. Paul's, Middleton—all in Lancashire; whilst in Yorkshire to the schools at York, Malton and Hemsworth set up by Archbishop Holgate, Tadcaster was added by Bishop Oglethorpe, and Guisborough by Bishop Purseglove. Schools created by London merchants in their birthplaces include Rugby and Oundle, Holt in Norfolk, Aldenham in Hertfordshire, Daventry in North-amptonshire, Market Bosworth in Leicestershire, Burn-sall and Coxwold in Yorkshire. And where individual founders were not forthcoming, schools were established by the joint endeavour of townspeople, as at Blackburn, Halifax and Wakefield.

To appreciate this spectacular extension of educational facilities, let us look at the relatively poor and remote area around Lancaster. Before the Reformation there were grammar schools at Lancaster, Preston and Kendal. Another appeared at Kirkham before 1551; but five were created in Elizabeth's reign, and three others shortly afterwards. This was an average of one new school every eight years, all endowed and therefore relatively securely established. In Yorkshire some 15 or 16 grammar schools were founded or endowed for the first time in Elizabeth's reign, when over a third of all charitable benefactions in that county went to education. 'There are not many corporate towns now under the Queen's dominion,' wrote an observer in 1577, 'that have not one grammar school at the least, with a sufficient living for a master and usher', and the schoolmaster Richard Mulcaster considered in 1581 that already in her reign more schools had been built than previously existed in all her realm. But the tide of new foundations actually reached full flood between 1610 and 1640 when there was, in Jordan's words, 'a prodigious outpouring' of wealth on education, almost as much as during the whole Elizabethan age.

These foundation schools, however, were by no means the only ones that existed. A feature of this time is the proliferation of private grammar schools, mainly kept by country clergy in their parsonages, and often sending boys to the universities. As yet these are an

84

unknown quantity, but though individually small and ephemeral they must in the aggregate have formed a considerable part of the total school provision, contributing significantly to the enormous expansion of educational opportunity.[70] Nevertheless, it was these new public endowed schools, together with those older ones which survived the Reformation, that constituted the more or less permanent part of such educational system as England had until the nineteenth century.

Characteristics of later-Tudor grammar schools

How then was a grammar school founded? The essential act was the provision of an endowment. This took the form of a grant of land, or a rent charge on land, yielding an annual income for a master's salary and sometimes for an usher's as well. If the property was vested in the master he was himself responsible for the leases and the administration of the income, and his salary might be a stipulated proportion of the annual yield. However, this was more often the responsibility of the trustees or governors, a number of townspeople or local gentry and clergy, nominated by the founder and renewed by co-optation or election: they appointed the master, who often received a salary fixed by the founder according to the price levels then prevailing. The founder's intentions for the conduct of his school might be prescribed in statutes, sometimes very minutely as a precaution against default or misfeasance.[71] To prevent any lapse and possible discontinuity careful provision was often made for appointing the master, who was usually required to be a graduate, perhaps ordained, and sometimes unmarried. From the statutes, and also from the contemporary writings of practising schoolmasters, like William Kemp's *The Education of Children* (1588) and John Brinsley's *Ludus Literarius* (1612), books especially written for the guidance of young and inexperienced masters, we can form a clear picture of the routine of an Elizabethan grammar school.[72]

Most striking of its features compared with schools as we know them was its small size. Some schools in the Elizabethan age contained over 100 or 150 boys, but probably most had only half that number, taught in one schoolroom by one master, single-handed, or aided by an usher. Classrooms were generally unknown until the later nineteenth century. According to their proficiency the boys sat on forms, usually six in number, arranged down the two long sides of the schoolroom. At the top end was a dais on which stood the master's chair and desk, whence he taught the upper school; down one side of the room towards the door sat the usher, teaching the younger boys in the lower school. In country districts the one-man school was the norm. Here, although the master made use of older boys to teach the little ones, his work must have been lonely and unremitting: he had no free periods to give respite; if he was ill and could find no substitute the school closed, so his income from fees ceased and penury threatened; on his recovery he had to get his pupils together again or his family starved. And in an age without pensions he taught until he died, unless he had a benefice to which he could retire.

Socially, the boys were mainly the sons of merchants, farmers and parsons, with a few from the county gentry and perhaps occasionally one or two sons of labouring men. Some burgesses' sons might be admitted free on the foundation, as perhaps all were
86

originally (hence the usual appellation 'free grammar school'); but as the tide of inflation rose fees had to be imposed on local boys as well as outsiders, and soon these furnished the greater part of the master's livelihood, and often the whole of the usher's. Besides quarterly fees (up to a shilling at Hull after 1579 and at Lincoln after 1584), 'entering pennies' were paid and at Michaelmas candles were brought by the boys to light the schoolroom during the dark winter days. Travel being slow and difficult, all boys who lived beyond walking or riding distance would have to be boarders near the school. This obvious fact reduces the force of Professor Jordan's point that in only two of his ten counties 'could a boy have lived at a distance of more than twelve miles from an available grammar school in which he might have found free tuition'; for this was much too far for daily travel and would have compelled boarding—and in any case free tuition was usually confined to local boys, sons of burgesses or parishioners. There were, however, no 'public' boarding schools in the modern sense : non-local boys would live with the master or with some neighbouring family. Eton, Winchester and Westminster, it is true, were the fashionable and aristocratic schools, boarding their foundationers, but all endowed grammar schools were public schools, and their reputations depended on nothing more than the standing of the master for the time being and the willingness of parents to send their sons to him.

Boys were expected to enter about 7 or 8 years of age, having learnt to read English at some A.B.C. or petty school in the town, or perhaps from the curate in country districts. Writing they learnt in the lower forms of the grammar school from a visiting scrivener;

or in towns they might attend a scrivener's writing school in out-of-school hours. From the mid-sixteenth century, curriculum, teaching method and organization tended to become standardized in grammar schools throughout the country. Their common aim was a simple one: to teach boys to write and speak the best Latin and to make them good Anglicans. Everywhere the staple diet was Latin grammar, writing of Latin epistles, themes and verses in imitation of the best classical authors, Latin conversation and orations; supplemented by practical religion, and in the upper forms later in the century by some Greek and occasionally Hebrew, depending on the master's own scholarship. Anything else that was learnt would be incidental. Thus from Elizabeth's reign the curriculum lost the practical, vocational relevance it had possessed when it subserved the training of priests and clerks, and the grammar school gave a liberal, cultural education more suitable for scholars and gentlemen.

From this exclusively linguistic and literary fare there was no relief in the form of organized games, or art, craft and music, though play acting was a feature of some schools. By our standards the day was cruelly long, lasting eight or ten hours, and beginning at 6 a.m. in summer, 7 a.m. in winter; and holidays, mainly at Christmas and Easter, totalled only four or five weeks in the year. For all but the verbally gifted this must have been dreary nourishment, and boys were driven to it by constant flogging and a brutality and ignorance of child nature that appals us now. 'The grammar school is a heavy and tedious school,' complained a writer in 1582, and perhaps only a minority of boys endured the full course of seven years. Most would leave early to be apprenticed to trade, the few who persisted would pass on at 15 or 16 to the university, the greater number of them eventually to become clergymen, an occasional one or two of the wealthier graduates going on to one of the Inns of Court, not necessarily to qualify themselves for the law but simply to round off their education before settling down to their responsibilities as country landlords and magistrates.

For some two hundred years no fundamental change took place in the geographical distribution of grammar schools, their teaching and routine, or their social rôle. With the universities they formed the most enduring and also the most conservative element in the English educational scene until the early nineteenth century.

2. STATE CONTROL THROUGH THE STATE CHURCH

The importance of capturing the minds of the young in order to advance Protestantism was recognized on the Continent by Luther and Calvin, no less than by the Jesuits in fighting to secure and restore Catholicism. In England, too, the schoolmaster was seen by the authorities as a most valuable ally in promoting the new Elizabethan Settlement, or alternatively as a potentially dangerous disseminator of opposition to it. For this reason he continued to be regarded no less than in pre-Reformation times as part of the ecclesiastical system, subject to the bishop's control, but with the bishop acting now as the agent of the state.

Episcopal licensing of schoolmasters

The main instrument of this, as in the middle ages, was

the licence, but conferred now in all cases by the bishop, not the cathedral chancellor. Curiously enough, no mention of licensing appears until Mary's reign when her injunctions to the bishops (1554) ordered them to 'examine all schoolmasters and teachers of children and, finding them suspect in any ways, to remove them and place Catholic men in their rooms'.[73] In Elizabeth's reign the episcopal licence became the principal means of enforcing the new Anglican compromise in the schools. The Queen's injunctions of 1559 forbad any man to teach unless with the bishop's licence granted after an examination of his 'learning and dexterity in teaching', 'sober and honest conversation' and 'right understanding of God's true religion'.[74] Evidently this was intended to eliminate not only Catholics but also any teachers who were considered academically or personally ill-qualified to defend the new religious establishment. Archbishop Young of York in 1564 examined 57 schoolmasters from all parts of his diocese, allowing some to teach Latin, some only English, and rejecting others altogether.[75]

As in the mediaeval Church, ecclesiastical discipline depended largely on the bishop's visitation of his diocese, canonically required in the first year of his translation and triennially thereafter. On these occasions, personally or by delegation, he sought out irregularities by means of oral examination, written interrogatories and inspection of titles, licences and faculties. Invariably, one article of inquiry by Elizabeth's bishops concerned the schoolmaster, whether teaching privately or publicly, and his religious opinions. 'Whether your schoolmaster be of sound religion' is the common form of the early inquiries. Some bishops, however, were more inquisitive. In the diocese of Worcester

Bishop Sandys asks 'Whether you have any school-master in your parish; and if you have, what is his name; and how long hath he been with you, and who gave him his licence to teach; what is his stipend, and whether he teach in private house or publicly.' Additionally, by Act of Parliament in 1563 schoolmasters were required together with certain other influential persons to acknowledge on oath the royal supremacy, and apparently the administration of this was also entrusted to the bishops. Accordingly, we find Bishop Parkhurst of Norwich inquiring of the clergy in his diocese in 1569 'whether your schoolmasters . . . have taken the oath to the queen's majesty'; but he seems to have been the only diocesan who asked about this. What the government in London ordered and what provincial England did were often two very different things; and the effectiveness of these and later anti-Catholic measures is an open question.

After 1570 the Church increased its vigilance as the fight against Catholicism intensified. The first canons of the new Church of England issued in 1571 laid down that 'it shall not be lawful for any to teach the Latin tongue or to instruct children, neither openly in the schools neither privately in any man's house, but whom the bishop of that diocese hath allowed and to whom he hath given licence to teach under the seal of his office'. Hereafter, diocesan visitation articles of inquiry become more standardized and also more searching. Even so, whether Catholic sympathizers or not, schoolmasters continued to teach unlicensed and apparently often went undiscovered—the bishop of Durham found 12 out of 24 in his diocese without licence in 1578. Accordingly in 1580, when the war against the Counter-Reformation was nearing its height, parliament supplemented the canon law by statutory penalties: by 'an Act to retain the queen's majesty's subjects in their due obedience' any person or corporate body keeping an unlicensed schoolmaster was liable to a fine of £10 a month, the schoolmaster himself to a year's imprisonment.[76] The detection of unorthodox or unreliable masters, however, seems to have continued mainly a responsibility of the bishops. Not all were as energetic as Bishop Overton of Coventry and Lichfield who in 1584, finding that 'obstinate untowardness in religion of divers young gentlemen doth argue a manifest and most intolerable corruption in their bringing up and in schoolmasters', cancelled all licences, ordered all masters to appear before his consistory court at Lichfield, examined them in their 'ability for learning' and 'soundness for religion', and refused licences to those found unsuitable. The others he licensed, but only to teach in a specified place, not 'throughout the whole diocese uncertainly'.

Throughout Elizabeth's reign the government remained conscious of the need to supervise the religious orthodoxy and political reliability of schoolmasters in view of their power to mould the opinions of the most influential members of the rising generation. The guarantees took permanent form in 1604. An Act of Parliament that year forbad any person to teach without the bishop's licence, and this was supplemented in the same year by the 77th canon of the Church of England which demanded, as a condition of the licence, subscription to the royal supremacy, the Book of Common Prayer, and the Thirty-nine articles.[77] The idea that the licence conferred a local monopoly persisted well into the eighteenth century: as late as 1731 Hull corporation contemplated legal action against a private and unlicenced schoolmaster teaching in opposition to the town's public grammar school. Although for a long time largely an empty formality, the need for the licence was not legally removed until the Endowed Schools Act of 1869.

The school as a means of propagating Anglicanism

In addition to the schoolmaster's doctrinal conformity, religious training of a uniform kind was enforced on schools in order to secure the new Establishment. This chiefly took the form of authorized manuals of religious instruction—the Primer for young children, the Catechism for older ones. The first Catechism specially for school use was issued by Edward VI's command in 1553, a Latin version being authorized for grammar schools. This last was superseded after 1570 by the Latin Catechism written by Alexander Nowell, dean of St. Paul's and a leading educationist of the time, the exclusive use of which was enjoined by the canons of 1571 and thereafter made the subject of routine inquiry by the bishops on visitation. Greek and English versions were soon produced, and in one form or another Nowell's Catechism was a standard text for over a century, the canon law prescription often being echoed in founders' statutes.[78]

This uniformity of religious instruction was reinforced by the compulsory use of the Royal Grammar. As early as 1529 a commission of churchmen had been appointed to recommend a standard method of grammar teaching based on the study of a single text; they chose the Latin grammar compiled *c* 1515 by William Lily and his collaborator Erasmus for St. Paul's school, and the sole use of this in a modified form had been commanded by proclamation of Henry VIII in 1542, whence its name the Royal Grammar. The royal injunctions of 1547 and 1559 and the canons of 1571 and 1604 also ordered its exclusive use, and the enforcement of this rule was similarly left to the bishops. Although in the course of time numerous rival Latin grammars were published, this one, later known as the Eton Grammar, remained in general use until Benjamin Hall Kennedy's *Latin Primer* appeared in 1866.[79]

To the compulsory teaching of the Catechism was added compulsory bible study and church attendance. The injunctions of 1559 ordered all teachers of children to 'stir and move them to love and do reverence to God's true religion now truly set forth by public authority' by having them learn 'such sentences of scripture as shall be most expedient to induce them to all godliness'.[80] To the same end the canons of 1571 commanded masters to accompany their scholars to church 'as often as any sermon shall be', afterwards examining them on what they had heard; and failure to attend church was punishable in the same way as unlicensed teaching under the Act of 1580. School statutes often supplemented the law to make corporate church attendance a routine part of school life. Thus, for example, at St. Albans in 1570 'the . . . schoolmaster and scholars shall every Sunday and Holy Day repair unto St. Albans church and there shall . . . sit together in the chancel or some other place of the church as the parson, churchwardens and schoolmaster shall agree'.[81] Every grammar school would have some part of the adjacent parish church set aside for the boys to occupy as a body when they attended with the master on days of public worship.

In these various ways Church and state endeavoured to regulate the schools in the interests of religious uniformity. By the 1570s every bishop on his visitation wanted to know if the local schoolmaster was duly licensed; if he taught the authorized grammar and catechism and appropriate sentences of scripture; if he regularly attended Holy Communion and took his scholars to church at sermon time. Under this surveillance the grammar schools must have played a significant part in achieving the transition of England from Catholicism to Protestantism in the short space of three or four decades, though it is a part seldom acknowledged by historians of the period. For the next two hundred years, confronted by this Anglican monopoly, Catholics were driven to defy the law and educate their children in secret or send them to schools maintained by English Catholics abroad.[82] Thus it was because of its historic rôle as guardian of education that the Church of England so jealously opposed the state and nonconformity when national education again became a political concern in the nineteenth century.

3. TRANSITION IN THE UNIVERSITIES

Even more than the grammar schools, the universities played a decisive rôle in advancing the Reformation. English protestantism was largely an academic movement, stemming particularly from Cambridge; thus Cambridge steadily grew in importance until by Elizabeth's reign its influence on national affairs far surpassed Oxford's. Both universities were profoundly affected by the Reformation, undergoing changes in their physical appearance, their studies, teaching and organization, and in their relations with state and society—changes which gave them a very different character by the end of the sixteenth century, and one which they retained almost unaltered until the mid-Victorian era.

The Dissolution: loss and gain

Already by c 1520 a small Lutheran group existed at Cambridge and heretical ideas were carried to Oxford by Cambridge scholars who were unsuspectingly imported by Wolsey into Cardinal College. At an early stage of the Reformation the universities were implicated, first in 1530 when their opinion on the legality of the king's marriage was invited, and then in 1534 when they were asked to pronounce on papal jurisdiction in England. But the first major impact of the Reformation came with the dissolution of the monasteries. In 1538 all four mendicant convents disappeared at both Oxford and Cambridge, to be followed over the next three years by the closure of all monastic houses of study, five at Oxford, one or two at Cambridge. But, as we have seen, monks and friars had for long played only a minor part in university life, and their departure was no irreparable loss. Indeed, in the long run, the Dissolution may be supposed an advantage.

For one thing, Henry VIII used some of the proceeds to found the grandest college in each university. After Wolsey's fall, Cardinal College at Oxford had become King Henry VIII College and in 1546 this was combined with the new cathedral church of Oxford to form Christ Church, the only college whose chapel is a cathedral. At Cambridge, also in 1546, the king used the site and buildings of King's Hall and Michaelhouse to create Trinity College, perhaps the noblest of all colleges. But the universities also gained by his foundation at Cambridge in 1540 and at Oxford in 1546 of five

Regius professorships of theology, medicine, civil law, Greek and Hebrew, each handsomely endowed with an annual stipend of £40.

Moreover, any damage suffered by the closing of monastic colleges was only temporary, for many of the buildings soon reverted to academic use. At Cambridge, Buckingham College was re-founded as Magdalene College as early as 1542 by Baron Audley, Henry VIII's Chancellor; the Carmelite friary was acquired by Queens' College in 1544, and the Franciscan friary later went to form Sidney Sussex College. At Oxford, Canterbury College became part of Christ Church; in Mary's reign the site and premises of Durham College were bought by a Catholic royal official, Sir Thomas Pope, to found Trinity College, and Sir Thomas White, a London merchant taylor, obtained St. Bernard's College to form St. John's College—the last college of the Old Religion; Gloucester College became a university hall in 1559 and survives as Worcester College; and the remains of St. Mary's College passed to Brasenose College in 1580.[83] Clearly then, so far as buildings are concerned, the Dissolution occasioned little injury to university education.

Much more grievous was the harm inflicted on scholarship, outside as well as inside the universities, by the wholesale dispersal or destruction of books and manuscripts in monastic libraries, a loss described as 'easily the greatest single disaster in English literary history'.[84] Not only were monastic libraries scattered, but 'popish' and 'superstitious' books were also cast out of university and college libraries: Thomas Cromwell's visitors in 1535 left the quadrangle of New College strewn with the leaves of 'Dunce' Scotus, 'the wynde blowyng them into everye corner'. Purged and repurged

97

by rival reforming factions, particularly in the reigns of Edward VI and Mary, the Cambridge library contained only 175 volumes in 1556; the Oxford library ceased to exist altogether, being re-founded by Sir Thomas Bodley with 2,000 volumes in 1602. After 1585 both universities had their licensed printers, but their output of books was comparatively small.

What is remarkable about the Dissolution in so far as it concerned the universities is not that so much was lost as that so much escaped. The Oxford and Cambridge college was in a sense, Professor Knowles says, 'the lowest species of the monastic genus', and it is a matter for surprise that both Henry VIII and Edward VI made an exception in its favour. 'Alone, and almost by accident, it escaped dissolution . . . and remained, with its shadow of a common life and with its society of celibate clerical fellows, almost till within living memory the sole surviving relic of the monastic middle ages.'[85]

State control to advance the state religion

In earlier centuries the universities had been quick to resist outside interference in their affairs; but during the Reformation they capitulated outright to the royal supremacy. Their subjection to the Crown and their use by it as instruments of ecclesiastical policy goes far to explain the relative ease with which the English Reformation was accomplished. The universities, observed the Privy Council in 1549, were 'the wells and fountains of religion within our realm'. There, far more than in the grammar schools, the minds of the rising generation of influential men, clergy and gentry, were shaped; and there, no less important, doctrine was refined in the theological polemics of scholars. For both these reasons the universities were early made to bow to the royal supremacy and converted into engines of the new Protestant orthodoxy.[86]

The Crown's main instrument of control was the royal visitation. The visitors were the king's commissioners empowered to examine all aspects of the universities' work, and then issue injunctions correcting and reforming whatever they considered necessary, so to ensure conformity with the religious policy then prevalent. Thomas Cromwell conducted the first visitation of both universities in 1535, to enforce the new royal supremacy over the Church, and to extirpate 'the papal usurpation'. Other visitations were held early in each of the three following reigns. Edward VI's visitors in 1549 sought to promote the reformed religion by expelling Catholics and eliminating 'popish superstitions'. Queen Mary's in 1556 restored Catholicism, burned heretical books and ejected Protestant heads and fellows of colleges. Queen Elizabeth's in 1559 reintroduced the Edwardian statutes, evicted Catholic dons and reinstated many of the Puritan ones displaced by Mary. Thus was unequivocally demonstrated the universities' subordination to the state and the principle of religious uniformity in the state's interest. However, direct royal interference on this scale ceased in Elizabeth's reign; the universities were kept in line by their respective chancellors, both powerful ministers of state (Lord Leicester at Oxford, Sir William Cecil at Cambridge, whilst individual colleges were disciplined by their official visitor, usually a bishop, or where necessary by special commissioners.

Yet another means of compelling academic conformity was by oaths and subscriptions, whether demanded by Act of Parliament or university statute. The first of these was imposed as early as 1536 when all candidates for degrees had to acknowledge the royal supremacy, and this was repeated by the Act of 1559. At Oxford, where recusancy was strong, the oath of supremacy was supplemented by religious tests, no person being admitted to a degree after 1576 unless he subscribed to the Thirty-nine articles of the Church of England; and this was extended in 1581 to all undergraduates of 16 and over. If the resultant exodus of Catholic dons and students impoverished Oxford to any extent, it benefited the new Jesuit colleges abroad, especially that at Douai in Flanders, where many English Catholics, in defiance of the law, now went to be educated. No religious tests were imposed at Cambridge, and advanced Puritanism flourished there, notably at St. John's College, powerfully affecting the new national Church. It was thus that in Elizabeth's reign Cambridge played its most dominant rôle in English intellectual life until the great age of experimental science in the twentieth century.

To assist the enforcement of religious orthodoxy no less than that of academic discipline, both universities began to keep matriculation registers—Cambridge in 1544, Oxford in 1565. Records were made of each student's name, age, residence, parentage, and social rank; they thus afford valuable evidence for social as well as educational history. At first, however, the registers were not kept with regular thoroughness, and considerable numbers of students appear to have avoided matriculation, perhaps in order to escape the oaths and subscriptions.[87]

University education was finally closed against non-Anglicans in the reign of James I when by royal command all candidates for degrees at Oxford and Cambridge were required to subscribe to the three articles in the 36th canon of 1562, acknowledging the royal supremacy, the Book of Common Prayer and the Thirty-nine articles. Thus, both universities were converted into twin strongholds of the Established Church, and so they remained until the late nineteenth century. Religious tests were not finally abolished until 1871, dons were almost invariably celibate clergymen until the 1880s, and compulsory chapel attendance survived until well into the present century.

Eclipse of the university by the colleges

Other developments in the Tudor period, which gradually transformed the mediaeval character and function of the universities, sprang directly or indirectly from the Reformation. Most fundamental was a change in the rôle of the colleges. From being small societies of privileged graduates supported in their higher studies by the founder's charity, they came to consist predominantly of undergraduates, most of them paying fees. Waynflete's statutes for Magdalen had recognized fee-payers in 1480, as had those for God's-house, Cambridge, in 1495. But by the mid-sixteenth century students not on the foundation ('commoners' at Oxford, 'pensioners' at Cambridge) came to be admitted at all colleges, partly perhaps at first to offset loss of revenue through inflation. This tendency was reinforced, however, by the rule that all students must reside in a college, so that their religious opinions could be more closely supervised in the interests of orthodoxy. At Oxford, where Catholics had preferred private lodgings in order to escape the tests, students were forbidden to live in ordinary houses in 1580. By the end of the century, all students at both universities belonged to a college. It was the colleges, indeed, that admitted students to the university: the university merely registered them, and this is still the case.

Meanwhile, harrassed by lack of endowments and falling student numbers in the troubled decades of the mid-century, the mediaeval hostels at Cambridge disappeared; at Oxford only eight halls survived in 1552, most of them later becoming adjuncts of neighbouring colleges—one only, St. Edmund Hall, still existing. In Elizabeth's reign, as residence became the rule and student numbers increased (there were some 3,000 in the two universities *c* 1575), more colleges were founded—the first of the Protestant era: Jesus (1571) at Oxford, Emmanuel (1584) and Sidney Sussex (1596) at Cambridge, the last two strongly Puritan and intended to increase the supply of preaching ministers. Hence, as the colleges grew in number, prestige and importance, the university as such shrank into comparative insignificance.

The university's eclipse resulted from another and simultaneous development in the college system. Early founders had never contemplated the education of the young, though some fifteenth-century colleges, notably Waynflete's Magdalen, had provided teaching for their own members. The mediaeval student had attended the public lectures of university regent masters, and the early sixteenth century saw the first permanent endowment of some of these—in 1502 the Lady Margaret Beaufort, mother of Henry VII, founded chairs of divinity at both Oxford and Cambridge, and these were followed by Henry VIII's public professorships of divinity, civil law, Greek, Hebrew and medicine. But public university lectures were soon to become relatively unimportant. Partly because of the multiplication of printed books and the creation of college libraries, more especially because of the growing predominance of the colleges as places of residence, teaching came to be concentrated there, each one providing for the instruction of its own students by college lecturers. On admission to a college, all undergraduates were assigned in ones or twos to a tutor, usually a fellow, who supervised their education, their morals and their finances until they took their B.A. In time, the education of undergraduates became the primary concern, teaching became the monopoly of the colleges, and university professorships became sinecures. The tutorial system, though now much changed, is often considered the most valuable and characteristic feature of Oxford and Cambridge education. How to adjust the respective rôles and powers of university and college, professor and tutor, in the best interests of teaching and research has been a fundamental problem of successive reform movements ever since the 1850s, and it still remains.

Changes in studies, students, government

Other changes in teaching and studies were taking place at this time. Grammar was discarded as a university subject. With the classical Renaissance and the growth of humanism Latin became more Ciceronian and so a dead language, known only by scholars; Greek and Hebrew were introduced; and, although Aristotle was not unseated till the age of Locke and Newton, the emphasis in the arts course tended to change from logic to rhetoric. The Reformation also saw the end of canon law, forbidden by Henry VIII's visitors in 1535. Even in the fifteenth century, because of the difficulties of maintenance, the number of higher degrees had fallen, but compared with the arts faculty the higher faculties of theology, law and medicine now shrank into insignificance, with the result that university education became much less professional than formerly.

The limited competence and vested interests of college tutors must have contributed to this end, but the principal reason undoubtedly was a change in the type of university student. Until c 1540 the student had been a tonsured clerk, destined for the service of Church or state in some capacity; by c 1580 he was as often as not a well-to-do young man without clerical or scholastic ambitions, interested chiefly in personal cultivation and gentlemanly accomplishments. As early as 1549, Bishop Latimer had complained, 'There be none now but great men's sons in colleges and their fathers look not to have them preachers.' Students of this kind formed the commoners and pensioners, those of higher social rank being admitted as 'noblemen' or gentlemen- or fellow-commoners, enjoying among other privileges exemption from such vulgarities as college lectures and exercises. So the cost of university education rose, and c 1600 a careful student probably needed £12 to £15 a year. 'Poor scholars' now entered as 'servitors' at Oxford, 'sizars' at Cambridge, performing menial services in return for the charity of the college, which was often supplemented by local or closed scholarships or exhibitions, limited to boys from particular schools or localities. The foundation of these was a characteristic sixteenth- and seventeenth-century benefaction: a college scholarship was often the only endowment a grammar school possessed apart from the master's salary.[88] Like their mediaeval predecessors, many of these poorer students made the Church their career. Thus, whilst remaining the seminaries of the Church of England, the universities underwent considerable laicisation; they also became much more the preserve of the rich and more class-conscious in their composition. Their function also came to be the education of young men whose studies stopped at or even before the B.A., few of whom had any intention of continuing to teach and study as regents. Consequently, the old scholastic curriculum had to be broadened to cater for the cultural education of gentlemen in a more secular and classical age. Also, as residence, lectures and disputations for higher degrees came to be dispensed with, the superior faculties languished, and they became a reality again only after the reforms of the late nineteenth century—the M.A. degree at Oxford and Cambridge is still only a formality, signify nothing more than the lapse of four years after the B.A. and the payment of a fee. One practice of the university long survived these changes: until well into the nineteenth century exercises for degrees continued to be conducted on mediaeval lines, orally and syllogistically and in Latin—the husks of mediaeval scholasticism, preserved by the force of academic conservatism.

Many of these tendencies, gathering force for a century or so, were stereotyped when the ancient statutes were revised and codified, at Cambridge in 1570, at Oxford not finally until 1636. So far as university government was concerned the new codes were revolutionary. Although the old legislative assemblies of regents and non-regents remained, the academic democracy of the mediaeval university was replaced by a close oligarchy of college heads, who not only had a veto but annually nominated from among themselves in rotation the vice-chancellor, the supreme administrative officer after the chancellor became a non-resident grandee. The colleges were thus made paramount: all that was left for the university to do was to conduct examinations and grant degrees, and both functions eventually became largely matters of form. This was the statutory situation which the mid-Victorian royal commissions had to reform before the modernization of the universities could begin.

However, if these constitutional developments tended in time to debilitate the universities, that was not so at first. Fed by more and more grammar schools the universities rose to numbers previously unap-proached—some 4,000 students in the 1630s. They were then probably fuller in relation to the population, and more closely representative of serious thought in the country, than at any time until the present century.

Notes

ABBREVIATIONS: *E.C.D.*—Leach, A. F., *Educational Charters and Documents*, Cambridge Univ. Press, 1911; *S.M.E.*—Leach, A. F., *Schools of Medieval England*, Methuen, 2nd ed., 1916; *V.C.H.*—*Victoria County History*.

1 Coulton, G. G., *Social Life in Britain from the Conquest to the Reformation*, Cambridge Univ. Press, 1918, pp. 57-58.
2 Purvis, J. S., *Educational Records*, York, St. Anthony's Press, 1959, p. 10.
3 *S.M.E.*, vii-ix gives a list of practically all of Leach's writings. Some of the most valuable are his chapters on schools in numerous volumes of *V.C.H.* Much used by school historians, *S.M.E.* has largely been ignored by professional scholars. Certainly it has to be used with caution, for sometimes its judgments are rash and its details unreliable, but it remains unsuperseded for the post-Conquest period.
4 Following Leach, these are the foundation dates still claimed by these schools.
5 Haskins, C. H., *The Renaissance of the Twelfth Century*, Harvard Univ. Press, 1927; but this should be supplemented by Southern, R. W., 'The Place of England in the Twelfth Century Renaissance', *History*, xlv (1960), 201 ff.
6 *E.C.D.*, 71
7 *E.C.D.*, 123, 143.

8 Edwards, K., *The English Secular Cathedrals in the Middle Ages*, Manchester Univ. Press, 1949, 187 ff.

9 *S.M.E.*, 115.

10 Edwards, *Secular Cathedrals*, p. 199.

11 *E.C.D.*, 233, 239, 253 ff.

12 Coulton, G. G., *Europe's Apprenticeship*, Nelson, 1940, p. 123.

13 *E.C.D.*, 331-41.

14 White, B. (ed.), *Vulgaria of John Stanbridge and . . . Robert Whittinton*, Early English Text Society, 1932, xvii-xx, xxi-xxiii.

15 *S.M.E.*, 206; *E.C.D.*, 321-29.

16 *S.M.E.*, 252-53, 257-60; *E.C.D.*, 405-15.

17 *E.C.D.*, 402, 418; *V.C.H. Oxford*, iii, p. 42 for the decay of grammar teaching at Oxford.

18 *V.C.H. Cambridge*, iii, p. 429.

19 White, *Vulgaria*, xvi ff.; Nelson, W. (ed.) *A Fifteenth-Century School Book*, Oxford Univ. Press, 1956, p. vi.

20 *S.M.E.*, 300-301.

21 *E.C.D.*, 315-17.

22 *E.C.D.*, 448-51.

23 Coulton, *Social Life*, pp. 264-65.

24 *E.C.D.*, 445-47.

25 *E.C.D.*, 101-109. For the disputed migration from Paris see Rashdall, H., *The Universities of Europe in the Middle Ages*, ed. Powicke and Emden, Oxford Univ. Press, 3 vols., 1936, iii, pp. 465-76.

26 *E.C.D.*, 141-43.

27 *E.C.D.*, 149-53.

28 *E.C.D.*, 155, 159-63.

29 *E.C.D.*, 165-69.

30 *E.C.D.*, 283-89.

31 Rashdall, *The Universities of Europe*, iii, p. 106. Until 1868 Oxford was policed at night by a force provided by the university.

32 Coulton, *Social Life*, pp. 55-56.

33 For the curriculum and exercises for the Oxford B.A. in 1267 see *E.C.D.*, 191-95. Responsions, the first of three examinations for the B.A., was abolished in 1960.

34 Jacob, E. F., *Essays in the Conciliar Epoch*, Manchester Univ. Press, 2nd ed., 1952, p. 222.

35 *E.C.D.*, 181-87 gives some of the Merton statutes of 1274.

36 *E.C.D.*, 223-31 for the foundation of Peterhouse.

37 *E.C.D.*, 349-73; *V.C.H. Oxford*, iii, 144 ff.

38 *V.C.H. Cambridge*, iii, 376 ff.; Coulton, *Social Life*, pp. 69-77 gives translations of some of the statutes of King's College. Students there took their B.A. without examination until 1851, at New College until 1834.

39 Nuffield College (1937), St. Anthony's (1950) and the newly planned Wolfson College are to some extent modelled on the All Souls plan, being mainly societies of fellows with some graduate students.

40 *V.C.H. Oxford*, iii, 195.

41 For Crown payments on behalf of scholars at King's Hall see Rickert, E., *Chaucer's World*, Oxford Univ. Press, 1948, p. 110.

42 Jacob, *Conciliar Epoch*, p. 213. Rickert, *Chaucer's World*, pp. 108-9 has examples of bequests for study.

43 Rashdall, *The Universities of Europe*, iii, 456.

44 Knowles, D. and Hadcock, R. N., *Medieval Religious Houses*, Longmans, 1953, pp. 9-41; also lists of houses for reference.

45 Knowles, D., *The Religious Orders in England*, Cambridge Univ. Press, ii, 1955, p. 294.

46 Some early rules of Westminster Abbey's almonry school are given by Rickert, *Chaucer's World*, pp. 116-117.

47 *S.M.E.*, 230; *E.C.D.*, xxxii.

48 For some of these grants see *E.C.D.*, 93, 95, 109, 117.

49 'The monk's duty is not to teach but to do penance', quoted by Coulton, G. G., *Monastic Schools in the Middle Ages*, London, published by the author, 1913, p. 4.

50 Rashdall, *The Universities of Europe*, iii, pp. 184-91, 295.

51 *E.C.D.*, 289-95; Knowles, D., 'English Monastic Life in the Later Middle Ages', *History*, xxxix (1954), 28.

52 Two late instances are given in *E.C.D.*, 439, 445.

53 Rashdall, *The Universities of Europe*, iii, p. 190.

54 Knowles, *Religious Orders*, iii, pp. 65, 92, 101-104.

55 Power, E., *Medieval English Nunneries*, Cambridge Univ. Press, 1922, p. 270.

56 Knowles and Hadcock, *Medieval Religious Houses*, p. 36.
57 Dickens, A. G., *The English Reformation*, Batsford, 1964 is the most authoritative recent general survey. For the European setting see the same writer's *Reformation and Society in Sixteenth-Century Europe*, Thames and Hudson, 1966.
58 *E.C.D.*, xii.
59 Simon, Joan, *Education and Society in Tudor England*, Cambridge Univ. Press, 1966. This large-scale work now provides the fullest study of the subject. Much the same field is covered by Charlton, Kenneth, *Education in Renaissance England*, Routledge and Kegan Paul, 1965.
60 *E.C.D.*, 453-69 gives the 1541 statutes of the King's School, Canterbury.
61 The Westminster School statutes (*E.C.D.*, 497-525) afford a detailed picture of one of the greater Elizabethan schools.
62 Dickens, *The English Reformation*, p. 150.
63 Dickinson, J. C., *Monastic Life in Medieval England*, Black, 1961, p. 132.
64 *E.C.D.*, 472-75, prints the Chantries Act of 1547
65 Leach, A. F., *English Schools at the Reformation*, Constable, 1896, pp. 5-6. This, Leach's early work, was based on previously unused chantry documents in the public records. Whilst it showed clearly that English schools did not begin with Edward VI, its argument about the 'spoilation' went beyond his own evidence.
66 Professor Dickens calculates that of 94 mediaeval hospitals in Yorkshire, 57 had vanished before 1500 (op. cit., p. 209). It may well be that many schools suffered a similar fate.
67 Jordan, W. K., *Philanthropy in England 1480-1660*, Allen and Unwin, 1959, p. 287.
68 See, for example, L. Stone's review of Jordan's book in *History*, xliv (1959) 257 ff.
69 Hoskins, W. G., 'Harvest and Hunger', *The Listener*, (10 Dec. 1964), 932.
70 Stone, L., 'The Educational Revolution in England 1560-1640', *Past and Present*, xxviii (1964), 41-80.
71 For some typical Elizabethan school statutes see in Carlisle, N., *Endowed Grammar Schools*, 2 vols., 1818;

those for Northwich, 1558 (i, 129); St. Albans, 1570 (i, 514); Sevenoaks, 1574 (i, 619); Dronfield, 1579 (i, 222); Sandwich, 1580 (i, 596); St. Bees, 1583 (i, 153); Hawkshead, 1588 (i, 656).

72 A massive study is by Baldwin, T. W., *William Shakspere's Small Latine and Lesse Greeke*, Univ. of Illinois, Urbana, 2 vols., 1944. For more elementary education see the same writer's *William Shakspere's Petty School*, Univ. of Illinois, Urbana, 1943.

73 Wood, N., *The Reformation and English Education*, Routledge and Kegan Paul, 1931, p. 54; and for reference Kennedy, W. P. M., *Elizabethan Episcopal Administration*, Alcuin Club, 3 vols., 1924.

74 E.C.D., 495.

75 Purvis, J. S., *Tudor Parish Documents*, Cambridge Univ. Press, 1948, pp. 103-109, gives details.

76 E.C.D., 526.

77 E.C.D., 528. Carter, E. H., *The Norwich Subscription Books*, Nelson, 1937, pp. 7-13 shows the development of subscription forms.

78 Watson, F., *The English Grammar Schools to 1660*, Cambridge Univ. Press, 1908, pp. 69-85.

79 E.C.D., 447; Watson, 243-59; also Baldwin, *Shakspere's Small Latine . . .* ii, pp. 690-701.

80 E.C.D., 495.

81 Watson, *English Grammar Schools*, pp. 45-49.

82 Much new information on this is given by Beales, A. C. F., *Education under Penalty*, Athlone Press, 1963.

83 Details in *V.C.H.* vols. cited.

84 Dickinson, *Monastic Life*, pp. 135-37.

85 Knowles and Hadcock, *Medieval Religious Houses*, pp. 44-45.

86 Wood, *The Reformation and English Education*, 105 ff.

87 Stone, 'Educational Revolution', 47 ff.

88 For scholarships see Jordan, *Philanthropy in England*, pp. 291-93, and (for local examples) his *Charities of Rural England 1480-1660*, Allen and Unwin, 1961.

Suggested Reading

BIBLIOGRAPHY

The most complete and up-to-date book lists are to be found in Simon, Joan, *Education and Society in Tudor England*, Cambridge Univ. Press, 1966.

SOURCES

These are indispensable for serious study. Leach, A. F., *Educational Charters and Documents*, Cambridge Univ. Press, 1911, is still the only collection covering this period. It should be supplemented by the relevant sections in Coulton, G. G., *Social Life in Britain from the Conquest to the Reformation*, Cambridge Univ. Press, 1918, pp. 43-99, and Rickert, E., *Chaucer's World*, Oxford Univ. Press, 1948, pp. 101-36.

SCHOOLS IN MEDIAEVAL ENGLAND

A brief introductory survey is Miner, J. N., 'Schools and Literacy in Later Medieval England', *British Journal of Educational Studies*, xi (1962), 16-27.
Leach, A. F., *The Schools of Medieval England*, Methuen, 2nd ed., 1916, was the pioneer study, and despite faults remains essential reading. Leach is reassessed by Simon, Joan, 'A. F. Leach on the Reformation', *British Journal of Educational Studies*, iii (1955), 128-43, iv (1955), 32-48, and by Chaplin, W. N., 'A. F. Leach: a Reappraisal', *British Journal of Educational Studies*, xi (1962), 99-124.

SUGGESTED READING

Watson, Foster, *The English Grammar Schools to 1660*, Cambridge Univ. Press, 1908, contains valuable information on school books and curriculum.
A useful approach to this subject is via individual school histories, but not all are equally reliable; for lists see Joan Simon's bibliography.

OXFORD AND CAMBRIDGE

Rashdall, H., *The Universities of Europe in the Middle Ages*, ed. Powicke, F. M. and Emden, A. B., Oxford Univ. Press, 3 vols., 1936, is still the standard authority; vol. iii deals with Oxford and Cambridge.
Consult also *Victoria County History of Cambridge*, vol. iii (The City and University) 1959, and *Victoria County History of Oxford*, vol. iii (The University of Oxford) 1954; each of these has a general historical account of the university, followed by short sections on the individual colleges.

THE MONASTIC CONTRIBUTION

There is no specialist study. Leach and Rashdall have relevant sections, and there are authoritative references *passim* in Knowles, Dom David, *The Religious Orders in England*, Cambridge Univ. Press, vol. i (1948), ii (1955), iii (1959). For the nuns' part see Power, Eileen, *Medieval English Nunneries*, Cambridge Univ. Press, 1922, ch. vi.

THE REFORMATION AND ENGLISH EDUCATION

Two recent works, both amply furnished with bibliographical references, now cover all aspects of this subject—Joan Simon's book mentioned above and Charlton, Kenneth, *Education in Renaissance England*, Routledge and Kegan Paul, 1965.
For a detailed but controversial argument for a post-reformation educational revolution see Jordan, W. K.,

Philanthropy in England 1480-1660, Allen and Unwin, 1959, pp. 279-97; and (for regional examples) the same writer's *The Charities of Rural England 1480-1660*, Allen and Unwin, 1961, pp. 52-60, 150-72, 299-360. Stone, Professor L., 'The Educational Revolution in England 1560-1640', *Past and Present*, xxviii (1964), 41-80 is an article of first-rate importance.

FURTHER READING

See other books and articles mentioned in the notes.